Corpus, Concordance, Collocation

DESCRIBING ENGLISH LANGUAGE

SERIES EDITORS

JOHN SINCLAIR · RONALD CARTER

Corpus, Concordance, Collocation

John Sinclair

lemma - headword as entered
into dictionary
build (built, building (?) ------)

Oxford University Press 1991

Oxford University Press
Walton Street, Oxford OX2 6DP

Oxford New York Toronto
Delhi Bombay Calcutta Madras Karachi
Petaling Jaya Singapore Hong Kong Tokyo
Nairobi Dar es Salaam Cape Town
Melbourne Auckland

and associated companies in
Berlin Ibadan

Oxford and *Oxford English* are trade marks of Oxford University Press

ISBN 0 19 437144 1

Typeset by Pentacor PLC, High Wycombe, Bucks
Printed in Hong Kong

To Angus McIntosh

Contents

4 Sense and structure in lexis

5 Words and phrases

6 The meeting of lexis and grammar

7 Evaluating instances

8 Collocation

9 Words about words

Contents

Acknowledgements

This book is dedicated to Angus McIntosh, who taught me English Language many years ago. His interest in vocabulary was infectious, and his farsightedness guided me into corpus work and computing in 1960.

The work would not have been possible without the co-operation of Collins Publishers and the University of Birmingham in the Cobuild project, now Cobuild Ltd. My evidence is largely cited from the Birmingham Collection of English Texts, donated by hundreds of copyright holders, who are listed in the front of Cobuild publications. It is based upon teamwork and years of discussion with colleagues in Cobuild, whose names, again, are featured on the individual publications.

To all of these I owe a profound debt of gratitude, and to my colleagues in the School of English, many of whom have taken a keen interest in the development of ideas about corpora and lexicology in the past decade.

One or two deserve specific mention for this book. Yang Hui-Zhong gave me a most useful framework for Chapter 2, and great encouragement in the early stages. Antoinette Renouf suggested the material for Chapter 4, and has worked closely with me on the design and management of corpora throughout the period covered by this book.

The description of *of* in Chapter 6 was built up over a number of presentations in the second half of 1988; at the TESOL Summer Institute of Flagstaff, Arizona, and at the BAAL Autumn meeting in Exeter, and with colleagues and students in Birmingham. I am grateful to Gwyneth Fox who helped me shape this chapter and the incorporation of grammar into the Cobuild approach. I am also grateful for the contributions of many generous people to this study.

In Chapter 7, I am particularly indebted to Jeremy Clear for his computing help, but his work pervades the whole book; also Tim Lane who implemented the computing for Chapter 8.

In the making of this book, I am indebted to Kay Baldwin for keying the manuscript, and to Geoff Barnbrook for arranging data transfers; to Elena Tognini Bonelli for reading the manuscript and making many helpful suggestions; and to David Wilson of OUP for his great care in controlling the process of publication.

Earlier versions of each chapter have been published separately, and I list the original sources below. All the original publishers have been contacted, and their co-operation in this publication is hereby acknowledged.

Acknowledgements

Chapter 1: *Language, Learning and Community*. C. N. Candlin and T .F. McNamara (eds.) 1989. National Centre for English Language Teaching and Research, Macquarie University, Sydney.

Chapter 2: *Computers in English Language Teaching and Research*. G. Leech and C. Candlin (eds.) 1986. Longman.

Chapter 3: *Dictionaries, Lexicography and Language Learning*. R. Ilson (ed.) 1985. ELT Documents No. 120. Pergamon Press/The British Council.

Chapter 4: *Linguistics in a Systemic Perspective*. J.D. Benson *et al*. (eds.) 1988. John Benjamins Publishing Company.

Chapter 5: *Looking Up*. J.M. Sinclair (ed.) 1988. Collins.

Chapter 6: *Learners' Dictionaries: State of the art*. M. L. Tickoo (ed.) 1989. SEAMEO REgional Language Centre, Singapore.

Chapter 7: *The English Reference Grammar*. G. Leitner (ed.) 1986. Niemeyer.

Chapter 8: *Language Topics*. Steele *et al*. (eds.) 1988. John Benjamins Publishing Company.

Chapter 9: *Linguistic Fiesta*. Yoshimura *et al*. 1990. Kurosio Publishers.

The author and series editors

John Sinclair has been Professor of Modern English Language at the University of Birmingham since 1965. His main areas of research are discourse (both spoken and written) and computational linguistics—with particular emphasis on the study of very long texts. He has been consultant/adviser to a number of groups including, among others, the Bullock Committee, The British Council, and the National Congress for Languages in Education. He holds the title of Adjunct Professor in Jiao Tong University, Shanghai. Professor Sinclair has published extensively, and is currently Editor-in-Chief of the Cobuild project at Birmingham University.

Ronald Carter is Professor of Modern English Language at the University of Nottingham where he has taught since 1979. He is Chairman of the Poetics and Linguistics Association of Great Britain, a member of CNAA panels for Humanities, and a member of the Literature Advisory Committee of The British Council. Dr Carter has published widely in the areas of language and education, applied linguistics, and literary linguistics. He is Director of the Centre for English Language Education at the University of Nottingham and is currently seconded part-time as National Co-ordinator for Language in the National Curriculum.

The author
and series editors

Foreword

Describing English Language

The *Describing English Language* series provides much-needed descriptions of modern English. Analysis of extended naturally-occurring texts, spoken and written, and, in particular, computer processing of texts have revealed quite unsuspected patterns of language. Traditional descriptive frameworks are normally not able to account for or accommodate such phenomena, and new approaches are required. This series aims to meet the challenge of describing linguistic features as they are encountered in real contexts of use in extended stretches of discourse. Accordingly, and taking the revelations of recent research into account, each book in the series will make appropriate reference to corpora of naturally-occurring data.

The series will cover most areas of the continuum between theoretical and applied linguistics, converging around the mid-point suggested by the term *descriptive*. In this way, we believe the series can be of maximum potential usefulness.

One principal aim of the series is to exploit the relevance to teaching of an increased emphasis on the description of naturally-occurring stretches of language. To this end, the books are illustrated with frequent references to examples of language use. Contributors to the series will consider both the substantial changes taking place in our understanding of the English language and the inevitable effect of such changes upon syllabus specifications, design of materials, and choice of method.

John Sinclair, *University of Birmingham*
Ronald Carter, *University of Nottingham*

Corpus, Concordance, Collocation

In this book, John Sinclair explores the implications of his most recent research into the language of extended texts, with particular reference to the lexico-grammatical patterns such research reveals. Throughout his career, John Sinclair has dedicated himself to the analysis of corpora of extended stretches of English language data. This book represents a natural extension of his work on discourse developed during the 1970s.

It is, however, fascinating to go back a decade further to the 1960s and re-read some of the articles he wrote at that time on lexis, lexical patterns, and computer-based processing of language. In 'Beginning the Study of Lexis' (published in 1966 in Bazell, C.E., *et al.* (eds.) *In Memory of J.R. Firth*), in particular, he identified theoretical and descriptive issues and developed ideas which have only recently begun to be brought to fruition. With the increased power of modern computers, the issues raised in this book set a fascinating agenda for the next decade. It is important, however, not to overlook the consistency with which, over several decades, and often working against the grain of prevailing orientations in the field, John Sinclair has approached such an agenda. *Corpus, Concordance, Collocation* represents simultaneously a culmination and a new beginning.

Ronald Carter

Introduction

Language study and the computer

This book charts the emergence of a new view of language, and the technology associated with it. Over the last ten years, computers have been through several generations, and the analysis of language has developed out of all recognition.

The big difference has been the availability of data. The tradition of linguistics has been limited to what a single individual could experience and remember. Instrumentation was confined to the boffin end of phonetics research, and there was virtually no indirect observation or measurement. The situation was similar to that of the physical sciences some 250 years ago.

Starved of adequate data, linguistics languished—indeed it became almost totally introverted. It became fashionable to look inwards to the mind rather than outwards to society. Intuition was the key, and the similarity of language structure to various formal models was emphasized. The communicative role of language was hardly referred to.

Although linguistics is gradually coming into balance again, it has left problems behind. Its most inward-looking period coincided with a surge of interest in computing, and a very limited type of computational linguistics became fashionable and remains the orthodoxy in many places.

This book offers an alternative. Throughout the decade of research reported, the basic method remains unchanged. Large quantities of 'raw' text are processed directly in order to present the researcher with objective evidence.

Thirty years ago when this research started it was considered impossible to process texts of several million words in length. Twenty years ago it was considered marginally possible but lunatic. Ten years ago it was considered quite possible but still lunatic. Today it is very popular.

The Cobuild project

Ten years ago, the English Language Research group at the University of Birmingham teamed up with Collins publishers, to investigate this

1

area and produce language reference works. During the 1970s, computational research on English had not progressed much in Birmingham because all the energy was spent on preparing for the future—devising software packages, instituting undergraduate courses, and influencing opinions on the campus. In particular, there was need to stress the growing importance of data-processing at a time when computing was almost confined to number crunching.

From 1980 to 1986, this essential preparatory work was put to good effect, and transformed through experience into a completely new set of techniques for language observation, analysis, and recording. The details are charted in a book called *Looking Up* (Sinclair, ed., 1988). A huge database of annotated examples was assembled, and a substantial dictionary edited from that (Sinclair *et al.*, 1987). Arising from another strand of research in Birmingham, the study of interactive discourse, innovations were made in the defining style, but the major novelty was the recording of completely new evidence about how the language is used.

The initial aims were modest, and no one anticipated that the project would have such a wide-ranging effect. The computer was thought of as having principally a clerical role in lexicography—reducing the labour of sorting and filing and examining very large amounts of English in a short period of time. In addition, the management of a long and detailed dictionary text made demands on conventional methods of book production, and in the late 1970s the prospects of computerized typesetting were growing more realistic.

It was not expected that the project would turn up anything very controversial. English, as the world's most described language, would not be likely to provide startling new evidence that had been overlooked for centuries; no provision was made in the plans for launching a new perspective on description.

Nevertheless, the design of the database was cautious, and the categories used to collect information were as neutral as could be devised at the time. Compilers were trained to note down the preponderant features that they observed, by selecting one or more typical examples and drawing attention to the critical features in each example.

As the evidence started to accumulate, it became clear that the accepted categories of lexicography were not suitable; the foundations of a new approach evolved during the dictionary project and have been supplemented since; these are outlined in the position statement below.

Three major areas of language patterning, besides grammar, could not be comprehensively presented in a dictionary, even an innovative one like Cobuild. These are *collocation*, *semantics*, and *pragmatics*. Collocation is the subject of current research, continuing a personal enthusiasm of the author. Semantic relationships are sketched out in the Cobuild dictionary, but the field is open for research that is not burdened with too many preconceptions. Pragmatics is often impossible to describe in relation to individual words, and needs separate research and treatment.

Cobuild has opened up a large range of research lines in the study and teaching of languages. The numerical and statistical side has hardly begun (though see Phillips 1989). Applications to language teaching through a lexical syllabus (Sinclair and Renouf 1988; Willis 1990) are now available and there is endless variety of detailed investigation to be done in the independent but parallel tradition established by Mindt (1988). Bilingual and multilingual research becomes possible as comparable corpora in other languages become available, notably in Italian, German, and Swedish, and the support of the Council of Europe in pioneering work is gratefully acknowledged. Experiments in new types of bilingual dictionary are in progress involving Brazilian Portuguese, and Arabic.

At the heart of all this activity lie a number of questions whose answers require reflection. The picture of language coming through is in crucial ways unlike what was expected. Is it wise to divide language patterning into grammar and something else (be it lexis or semantics or both) before considering the possibility of co-ordinated choice? Should we have confidence even in the assumption that discrete units of text, such as words, can be reliably associated with units of meaning? How do we represent the massive redundancy of language, which is often asserted but does not appear prominently in popular models of language?

These are fairly fundamental questions, which suggest that we should not jump into new theoretical positions until a great deal more research has been done, using the powerful new tools at our disposal.

Position statement

It is clear from the above that any position statement at the present time must be regarded as provisional. Nevertheless, it is worth making a statement every few years in times of swift change, so that the movement of ideas can be charted.

Accept the evidence

First and foremost, the ability to examine large text corpora in a systematic manner allows access to a quality of evidence that has not been available before. The regularities of pattern are sometimes spectacular and, to balance the variation seems endless. The raw frequency of differing language events has a powerful influence on evaluation.

The comprehensive nature of simple retrieval systems is an excellent feature. No instance is overlooked, and the main features of usage are generally clear. Minor patterns remain in the background. Some very common usages are often not featured in descriptions because they are so humdrum and routine; this method brings them to the fore. Especially in lexicography, there is a marked contrast between the data collected by computer and that collected by human readers exercising their judgement on what should or should not be selected for inclusion in a dictionary.

Indeed, the contrast exposed between the impressions of language detail noted by people, and the evidence compiled objectively from texts is huge and systematic. It leads one to suppose that human intuition about language is highly specific, and not at all a good guide to what actually happens when the same people actually use the language. Students of linguistics over many years have been urged to rely heavily on their intuitions and to prefer their intuitions to actual text where there was some discrepancy. Their study has, therefore, been more about intuition than about language. It is not the purpose of this work to denigrate intuition—far from it. The way a person conceptualizes language and expresses this conceptualization is of great importance and interest precisely *because* it is not in accordance with the newly observed facts of usage.

Reflect the evidence

The integrity of actual instances is a matter that has grown in importance during the period reported in this book. Most descriptive linguists with any field experience are disposed to record examples carefully and are cautious about accepting words, phrases, or sentences which have not been attested. However plausible an invented example might be, it cannot be offered as a genuine instance of language in use.

In the climate of the 1970s, this kind of position seemed pedantic, but from the very beginning of the research it was established that examples were not to be tampered with, and that every observation about the language was to be accompanied by at least one clear example of it. Gradually a mood of considerable humility developed, as it was realized how intricately constructed each example was. Even what seemed to be innocuous changes prompted by the need to clarify a point, led to the resultant adaptation being challenged.

There are, of course, plenty of bizarre and unrepresentative instances in any corpus—in fact, one really enlivening feature of corpus study is the individuality of examples. There are also instances which do not easily detach from their contexts, or which require a very extensive stretch of text to avoid distortion. The problem of finding and identifying typical examples is a particular research focus at present. However, the difficulties should not be allowed to support the absurd notion that invented examples can actually represent the language better than real ones.

This stance with respect to real examples still appears to be controversial. For many applied linguists, to abandon the practice of inventing or adapting examples would mean a big change; the demise of cherished methods and the wholesale revision of many publications. There is evidence now that re-assessment is beginning. In time, it will be realized that there is just no reason or motivation to invent an example when one is knee-deep in actual instances (and in the days of paper print-out the phrase 'knee-deep' was not always figurative!)

Natural language

What is more, the growing respect for real examples led in the mid-1980s to a notion of textual well-formedness, which was dubbed *naturalness* (Sinclair 1984). Any instance of language depends on its surrounding context. The details of choice shown in any segment of a text depend—some of them—on choices made elsewhere in the text, and so no example is ever complete unless it is a whole text. Invented examples would, therefore, appeal for their authenticity to a non-existent context, which would eventually be evaluated by someone's intuition, with all the misleading consequences of that.

The position of those who like to invent examples would be more plausible if, in practice, it was felt that they did a good job of simulation. However, it seems that sensitivity to context is very difficult to achieve, and even experts at simulating natural language are prone to offer examples which are extremely unlikely ever to occur in speech or writing.

If we accept that the requirements of coherence and communicative effectiveness shape a text in many subtle ways, the term *naturalness* is simply a cover term for the constraints that determine the precise relationship of any fragment of text with the surrounding text. It is again a position of some humility. Until a great deal more research has been done, we will not know exactly what naturalness relations consist of. Until then, we should be very careful not to misrepresent a language, and in particular, we should never offer as an instance of language in use, some combination of words which we cannot attest in usage.

The term naturalness is chosen to be deliberately contentious, because the phrase 'natural language processing' has for some years been used to describe a branch of computer science which did not feature the language of naturally-occurring texts. Currently, there are signs of a growing recognition that the comprehensive study of language must be based on textual evidence. One does not study all of botany by making artificial flowers.

Units of meaning

Our appreciation of the relation of meaning to form has developed considerably in the last decade. It first of all seemed rather a coincidence that very often a particular grammatical or lexical choice was found to correlate with one meaning of a word rather than another. Perhaps a verb tense, a word order, a prepositional choice, or a collocation would be there in a large number of cases.

Students of grammar are often victims of the 'all or nothing' argument, which does not allow a few exceptions to a pronounced tendency. Students of lexis in the early days were made to feel that this kind of statistical evidence was somehow not as good as the wholesome, contrived rules of grammar. Now it is manifest that the nature of text is not to follow clear-cut rules, but to enjoy great flexibility and innovation.

This is leading to wholesale changes in the idiom of language description. In the relation of form and meaning, it became clear that in all cases so far examined, each meaning can be associated with a distinctive formal patterning. So regular is this that in due course we may see formal patterns being used overtly as criteria for analysing meaning, which is a more secure and less eccentric position for a discipline which aspires to scientific seriousness. Once again, the stranglehold of intuition is being relaxed.

The models of meaning that we are 'given' by linguistic tradition are the dictionary and the thesaurus. The traditional dictionary cheerfully represents words as often having several discrete meanings, but gives no help whatever as to how in practice the language user distinguishes among them—how a writer can be fairly sure that the meaning he wants to signal is the one which will be understood, and vice versa.

The thesaurus operates in a different way, grouping together words which share similar meanings. Its organization is entirely abstract and conceptual (and mysterious to most users). No justification is given for groupings, and hardly any discrimination is made among members of long lists of words and phrases which ostensibly mean the same thing.

The recognition that form is often in alignment with meaning was an important step, and one that cut across the received orthodoxy of the explanation of meaning. Soon it was realized that form could actually be a determiner of meaning, and a causal connection was postulated, inviting arguments from form to meaning. Then a conceptual adjustment was made, with the realization that the choice of a meaning, anywhere in a text, must have a profound effect on the surrounding choices. It would be futile to imagine otherwise. There is ultimately no distinction between form and meaning.

From this kind of progression, there is no going back. The dictionary must adapt to new criteria of explicitness and accountability to evidence, and the thesaurus is due for complete overhaul and redesign.

Working with lexicographers made it clear that there are no objective criteria available for the analysis of meaning, and that in practice the observable facts of usage tend to be undervalued. Specific training in perceiving the patterns of language is required, and the example of the computer is valuable in stressing the difference between the text as a physical object, and the way it is perceived by a language user.

More recently, the whole idea of discrete units of meaning is called into question by new evidence. No doubt, a new kind of discrete or at least discernible unit will emerge from this re-examination, possibly more abstract than the kind of unit that linguists are accustomed to. At present, the mood is somewhat negative, because once again some long-held points of view are coming under attack.

One such point of view is in the area of morphology, and the process of lemmatization. It is now possible to compare the usage patterns of, for example, all the forms of a verb, and from this to conclude that they are often very different one from another. There is a good case for arguing that each distinct form is potentially a unique lexical unit, and that forms should only be conflated into lemmas when their environments show a certain amount and type of similarity.

The other is in the vexed area of idiom and lexical items which apparently consist of more than one word. No reliable method has yet been found for circumscribing these and isolating them from their context, which is the first prerequisite for conventional linguistic description. The evidence set out in this book continually stresses the intricate patterns that knit a text together. The role of grammatical choices as indicating meaning is becoming more and more suspect.

A new perspective, and one which fits in with the direction of current speculation, is the following: decisions about meaning are made initially at a very abstract level, and also in very broad and general terms. At that point there is no distinction between meaning and strategy. A new-born communicative intent passes through various stages of realization, during which decisions about expression begin to be taken. These have lexical and grammatical ramifications, and are moved towards final form through a series of default options, unless a specific effect is specified in the design. The default options embody the rules of grammar (and the less explicit but very obvious rules of collocation). Grammar is thus part of the management of text rather than the focus of the meaning-creation.

In this view of language, emphasis is placed on large and fairly inaccessible decisions about topics, message design, and strategies, and it is hoped that it will stimulate a new wave of theoretical studies. It has never been anticipated that a close study of text will solve the problems of description, but merely that it will indicate more clearly what problems there are to solve. The challenge to speculation and abstract inventiveness is growing as our ability to organize the data becomes more secure.

All in all, it looks as if linguistics has concentrated on much too narrow an area of study. First of all, by leapfrogging many questions concerning the physical manifestations of language (leaving phonetics and speech technology some serious problems) linguistics becomes too abstract too quickly. Second, by trying to account for all the meaning in language at levels only one step more abstract than the initial step that establishes the units, linguistics remains not abstract enough. Third, by working upwards from very small units like phonemes and letters, linguistics hardly ever gets to whole texts of any length and complexity, and where it does it seems unable to maintain connection between the large units and the small ones.

Guide to the contents of this book

The first two chapters give guidance and advice on the practicalities of getting started in corpus linguistics. The foundation of this technique is the corpus, and Chapter 1 deals in general with corpus creation. Particular efforts in building corpora are referred to in the Bibliography. The results are only as good as the corpus, and we are at a very primitive stage of understanding the character of corpora and the relation between decisions on the constitution of the corpus and information about the language derived from the corpus.

In the early 1980s, as the multi-million word corpus became available for study, it became clear that the whole idea of a corpus of finite size was flawed. Any corpus is such a tiny sample of a language in use that there can be little finality in the statistics. Even the projected billion-word corpora of the 1990s will show remarkably sparse information about most of a very large word list.

The idea of a *monitor corpus* was born. Sources of language text in electronic form would be fed on a daily basis across filters which retrieve evidence as necessary. The proposal for a monitor corpus is expounded in Chapter 1; the first monitor corpus is taking shape in Birmingham as I write.

Chapter 2 goes into the basic processing in some detail. There are now some quite powerful concordancing packages becoming available for domestic computers, and it is valuable for users to have an understanding of how they work and what the main options are. The chapter articulates a demonstration package put together by one of the pioneers of text processing in the East—Professor Yang Hui-Zhong of Shanghai.

The central chapters of the book together report a series of studies of concordances, which in various ways, show how the corpus evidence can stimulate new linguistic hypotheses.

An early speculation was that the correspondence between observable patterns and distinctions of meaning and use might be much greater than was generally supposed. The likelihood of this was initially ridiculed, but gradually evidence accumulated. In Chapter 3, the proposal is put in its simple form; in Chapter 4 an analysis is attempted of a word that offers many subtly different meanings, and Chapter 5 combines a general discussion of phrasal verbs with a study of *set* which moves towards an explanation of the interaction between word-choice and context.

The movement from vocabulary words such as *decline* and *yield* to common, hardly lexical words like *set* and *in*, continues in Chapter 6. This includes a consideration of how grammars will be affected by the new evidence. Early, rather simplistic speculations about large corpora took the line that since grammar dealt with frequently repeated events involving very common words, it would be well served by fairly modest corpora. The big numbers were only necessary for capturing rare lexis.

There are all sorts of reasons why this position is untenable, and in Chapter 6 a new method for moving from particular to general is proposed and illustrated. The Cobuild grammar offers a broad picture of English grammar (Sinclair, Fox *et al.* 1990). These studies raise serious matters about the treatment of individuality and generality in this kind of language study. Every instance is unique, and yet contributes something towards the total picture.

Chapter 7 points out that most of the textual evidence is actually problematic, and raises the intriguing question of evaluation—some instances are better for some purposes than others.

The distillation of the typical behaviour of a word—its collocations—is at the centre of this research. The Bibliography will trace the development of the notion that a language has a viable and interesting lexical structure based upon the tendencies of words to attract and repel each other—for whatever reason. This is my own research thrust, and after many years of patient inching forward, it is a real pleasure to report progress in Chapter 8. Work is now advanced on a first dictionary of collocations (Sinclair *et al.* forthcoming).

The final chapter is (as all final chapters should be) a beginning rather than an end. Two of the main ideas that have arisen from this research are:

a. the way we use language about language is much more important than is usually allowed for;

b. if a dictionary definition is written in ordinary English, all the subtle inferences and implications can be harnessed to improve the definition.

Expertise in the structure of language is now becoming central in information science, and grammars and dictionaries are as important for machines as for human beings. I have begun to try to understand the structure of ordinary language about language, and Chapter 9 is the first report on this.

The book is only a very small selection of the material produced in this exciting decade. But it makes a coherent account of the developments, and brings us right up to the present day.

1
Corpus creation

Introduction

The beginning of any corpus study is the creation of the corpus itself. The decisions that are taken about what is to be in the corpus, and how the selection is to be organized, control almost everything that happens subsequently. The results are only as good as the corpus.

Who should design a corpus?

Some features of the source are worth controlling, in a common-sensical way. The specification of a corpus—the types and proportions of material in it—is hardly a job for linguists at all, but more appropriate to the sociology of culture. The stance of the linguist should be a readiness to describe and analyse any instances of language placed before him or her. In the infancy of the discipline of corpus linguistics, the linguists have to do the text selection as well; when the impact of the work is felt more widely, it may be possible to hand over this responsibility to language-orientated social scientists. Certainly the bulk of any lay discussion about corpora concerns the criteria for text selection.

Until we know a lot more about the effects of our design strategies, we must rely on publishing a list of exactly what is in a corpus (for example, Renouf 1987). Users and critics can then consider the constitution and balance of the corpus as a separate matter from the reporting of the linguistic evidence of the corpus.

I outline below, in the most general terms, the considerations that are relevant to the creation of a corpus of texts.

A general corpus

The first consideration is the aim of the activity of corpus creation. It may be fairly general in providing a good selection of instances of the language for a variety of purposes, which do not need to be enumerated. Or it may be specific, as a stage in the development of a product or in the pursuit of a research goal. I shall highlight the construction of general corpora in this chapter, but the application to special needs should be shaped by similar considerations.

The value of a general corpus as a place of reference is very great, and likely to grow dramatically in the coming years. It is now accepted that the documentation of a language, in dictionaries, grammars, etc. is an essential stage in its maturation. More and more people in every branch of information science are coming to realize that a corpus as a sample of the living language, accessed by sophisticated computers, opens new horizons.

Outline of corpus creation

The creation of a corpus is a simple matter in outline. A decision is taken on a convenient size, and on priorities for selection, then by consulting catalogues, and so on, the text is picked for inclusion. Each of these steps will be discussed below, but there are two strictly practical matters that overshadow them.

Electronic form

One is that a computer-held corpus has to have the material in electronic form, either from print or obtained direct from a text-processing activity which uses computers (printing, word processing, electronic mail, etc.). There are three normal methods of text input at the present time:

a. adaptation of material already in electronic form;
b. conversion by optical scanning (machine reading);
c. conversion by keyboarding.

Most projects will make use of all three methods, since each is suitable for a different class of material. For example, handwritten material and transcriptions of spoken language will require keyboarding, and newsprint can only be economically included if it is available in electronic form. For the mass of books printed by conventional methods, scanning is much the best alternative. Since omnifont scanners (capable of reading any type-face) are still fairly rare and expensive, it is important for project managers to encourage their use, so that they will become more popular and accessible to the average user.

14

Scanners will always have value because so much print material will never be re-keyboarded. However, with modern methods of printing and publishing, there is nearly always an electronic stage. The originators of the text see this stage merely as a means to an end and rarely keep copies; the researcher should be able to secure co-operation and acquire more and more print material.

Permissions

The other practical problem is the securing of permission to put the text into electronic form, and to quote selections of it in various papers, reports, and other publications. This is a sensitive area of law and, although one experiences almost unfailing good sense from rights editors, the labour of keeping a large corpus in good legal health is enormous. It is likely that if copyright holders understood precisely why their texts were desired, and what safeguards there could be against exploitation and piracy, it would be possible to bypass this largely unproductive labour.

Until this problem is solved internationally, it is likely to get worse. Some advice can be given in particular instances, but corpus projects should be designed with this in mind as a potential shadow over the enterprise. There are signs that the Council of Europe is alert to this problem and may use its influence to further corpus creation in the languages of Europe. Publishers who have an interest in reference material are contemplating amendments to the normal authorial contract, so that in future there may be fewer legal problems and less unnecessary paperwork.

Design

With these practical matters clearly understood, we can turn to the criteria for selection of texts. In the main, this is applied common sense, but there are some reflections from experience that may be worth considering.

Spoken and written language

Perhaps the most far-reaching decision is whether the corpus will contain only written texts, or only spoken transcriptions, or both. Most corpora keep well away from the problems of spoken language

15

—with some honourable exceptions—and, for a corpus which in any way purports to reflect a 'state of the language', this is most unfortunate. Many language scholars and teachers believe that the spoken form of the language is a better guide to the fundamental organization of the language than the written form; and many writers comment on the differences. In my own experience, there is no substitute for impromptu speech, and a decision I took in 1961 to assemble a corpus of conversation is one of the luckiest I ever made. Even at that time, I was assured that an automatic transcription of speech was 'just around the corner'. It still is.

Quasi-speech

If it is impossible in an early stage of a project to collect the spoken language, then there is a temptation to collect film scripts, drama texts, etc., as if they would in some way make up for this deficiency. They have a very limited value in a general corpus, because they are 'considered' language, written to simulate speech in artificial settings. Each has its own distinctive features, but none truly reflects natural conversation, which for many people is the quintessence of the spoken language. There is special integrity in a text which is a full record of a public meeting, enquiry, court case, radio or television station, etc., despite the mix of impromptu and considered language that is used— scripts and even read-out statements are common. But such records are not likely to be representative of the general usage of conversation.

The creation of a spoken corpus is not as straightforward as that of a written one, and would require a chapter on its own. Since most corpus activity concerns the written language, I shall concentrate on that in the remainder of this chapter.

Formal and literary language

The material will range from formal to informal, from literary to ordinary. The formal will be easier to acquire than the informal, and the literary will be more easily noticed than the ordinary. In general, corpus designers should compensate for this fact. Ephemeral, and usually informal, written communications are sent through the post, pushed through the letter-box, left in piles in shops, offices, and waiting-rooms, added to packages and piled in our office in-trays in increasing profusion. They are often socially negligible, but they are widespread and typical of mundane prose.

Equally, it is not necessary to embellish the corpus with all the best pieces of contemporary literary writing. A small amount will suffice. The reason is simple and not at all sinister or anti-literary.

Typicality

One of the principle uses of a corpus is to identify what is central and typical in the language. This is most valuable as a place of reference against which the work of literary artists can be seriously studied. However, if the work of established writers was already dominant in the corpus, it would have little or no value as a point of normative reference. Further, it is characteristic of literature to innovate, and we may expect a corpus of literary texts to have a low proportion of ordinary, everyday English. And since the processing emphasizes repeated patterns at the expense of unique ones, most of the distinctive literary patterning would be lost, because it would not occur often enough to count as central and typical.

Equally, in journalism the well-known writers tend to have unusual ways of writing, and the more mundane and humdrum sorts of reporting will be more useful in the corpus.

This is a minefield of prejudice and misunderstanding. If we are to approach a realistic view of the way in which language is used, we must record the usage of the mass of ordinary writers, and not the stray genius or the astute journalist.

Design criteria

There are many other criteria that can be applied—too many in fact, because each criterion adds substantially to the number of different samples to be obtained. More on this point below. A discussion of most of the relevant criteria can be found in Renouf (1984), and in the same paper there is a record of the criteria used in the Cobuild project.

As a guide, I recommend for a general corpus that any specialized material is either kept out or stored separately as an ancillary corpus. A general reference corpus is not a collection of material from different specialist areas—technical, dialectal, juvenile, etc. It is a collection of material which is broadly homogeneous, but which is gathered from a variety of sources so that the individuality of a source is obscured, unless the researcher isolates a particular text.

17

The diversity of sources is an essential safeguard, until such work as Biber's (1988) categorizations using internal linguistic criteria has advanced sufficiently to allow efficient sampling. Now that newsprint is available in quantity, it must be remembered that the language of newspapers is just one variety of English—of one group of related varieties—and not a reliable sample of the language.

Period

Most corpora attempt to cover a particular period of time, and use the clearest time indicator, which is the time of first utterance or publication. However, if we are trying to sample the material that society has in front of it, then other factors become important. A written work may take some time to establish itself, and may remain influential for some time. The phraseology of Shakespeare and the King James Bible still exert an influence on present-day English usage.

Overall size

The dimensions of a corpus are of prime concern to most researchers in the initial conceptualization, and in the public statements. In the long run, they matter very little. The only guidance I would give is that a corpus should be as large as possible, and should keep on growing. This advice is based on the pattern of word occurrence in texts, first pointed out by Zipf (1935). Essentially, there is a huge imbalance in the frequency of the words. Most of any text is taken up by words like *of, is, up,* and *by*; rather less by *like, taken, any,* and *most*; still less by *words,* less again by *text* (the example words are the first ten words of this sentence). About half of the vocabulary of a text—even a very long text—consists of words that have occurred once only in that text.

The relation between words and their frequency is regular. The commonest word in English—*the*—has approximately twice the frequency of the next two, *of* and *and*. This is shown in Figure 4 of Chapter 2 (see Appendix I, located at the back of the book). The frequency drops sharply and fairly steadily, so that the nineteenth most frequent word, *be*, has less than ten per cent of the frequency of *the*, and the eighty-fourth word, *two*, has less than five per cent.

In order to study the behaviour of words in texts, we need to have available quite a large number of occurrences. Again the statistics are against us, since if we classify the occurrences in terms of 'uses' or 'meanings' we shall find the same kind of imbalance again. One of the uses will typically be twice as common as all the others; several will occur once only, and that is not enough on which to base a descriptive statement. This is why a corpus needs to contain many millions of words.

Sample size

The other decision that is needed at the outset concerns a suitable size for any sample. Opinions differ rather sharply. Some corpora—following the Brown (Brown University) corpus that opened up this kind of study, and its UK counterpart the LOB (Lancaster–Oslo–Bergen) corpus—opt for an even sample size, around 2,000 words, (Hofland and Johansson 1986). This has some advantages for comparison, and would be of value if the rest of the organization was also devised with attention to statistical factors. However, the major divisions of the corpus are into genres, identified on largely intuitive criteria. Also, a corpus which does not reflect the size and shape of the documents from which it is drawn is in danger of being seen as a collection of fragments where only small-scale patterns are accessible. See the section on sample corpora later in this chapter.

Whole documents

The alternative is to gather whole documents. Then there is no worry about the marked differences that have been noted between different parts of a text. Not many features of a book-length text are diffused evenly throughout, and a corpus made up of whole documents is open to a wider range of linguistic studies than a collection of short samples. There is no worry, either, about the validity of the sampling techniques.

Further, if for some reason it is desirable to have random samples—each of, say, 2,000 words, this is readily achievable from a large collection of complete texts. Here is another reason for advocating a policy of continuous growth: from a large corpus can be drawn any number of smaller, more specialized ones, according to requirements from time to time.

The penalties to pay for including whole documents are that in the early stages of gathering, the coverage will not be as good as a collection of small samples and the peculiarities of an individual style or topic may occasionally show through into the generalities. As against these short-term difficulties, there is a positive gain in the study of collocation, which requires very large corpora to secure sufficient evidence for statistical treatment.

Minimal criteria

There are a large number of possible criteria that can be used in selection. Hence, the advice on corpus creation is to agree the smallest set of criteria that can be justified in the circumstances, so that the number of different documents is as small as possible. It is advantageous to keep detailed records of the material so that the documents can be identified on grounds other than those which are selected as formative in the corpus. Then, the attempt is made to find a suitable document for each combination of criteria. The size is noted, and some or all of it may be entered in a corpus. Useful criteria for a general corpus include: whether the work is fiction or non-fiction; book, journal, or newspaper; formal or informal; and the age, sex, and origin of the author.

Provisional corpus

Using this procedure, there should be a useful small general corpus to be located somewhere between ten million and twenty million words. If some provisional analysis is desired, the corpus can be trimmed for the purpose, so that the criteria are roughly balanced. Trimming involves adding extra texts where there are gaps, and putting to one side portions of very long texts that over-emphasize one kind of writing. This kind of corpus will be adequate for the study of the fairly frequent patterns and meanings of many thousands of words, but will not be adequate for a reliable description of the language as a whole.

The size might then be increased, keeping to the same criteria, and a much clearer and more detailed picture be found. But still there will be thousands and thousands of loose ends—infrequent words, infrequent meanings, rare but distinctive phrases, sub-types of style, etc. For the study of collocation and phraseology, it is necessary to study huge amounts of text in order to isolate the recurrent patterns and reduce the prominence of the transitory ones. Recent work on grammar (Sinclair, Fox *et al.* 1990) suggests that the detailed patterns of individual words are necessary evidence on which to base the generalizations of grammar.

Processing

The strategy for holding, processing, and retrieving information from such a corpus needs a few words.

It would be helpful to agree on standard practices in the representation of text in a computer. At the time of writing, an international Text Encoding Initiative is in progress, devising conventions for text storage which will be much more sophisticated than most current conventions, and which may well lead to standardization in the near future. It is to be hoped that the Text Encoding Initiative will specify such things as:

a. full 'bibliographic' information to be provided, perhaps both in electronic form and on paper;
b. the actual language text to be separated from all other codes by a standardized convention;
c. language text to be coded in a widely recognized format, or details provided so that it can be converted easily;
d. any codes, other than those of running text, to be identified and classified, for example, into type-face codes, layout specifications, reference systems, housekeeping, language-analytic marks; full keys to non-standard codes to be provided; and in the description the difference to be made clear between automatic criteria and those mediated by human agencies.

Clean-text policy

The safest policy is to keep the text as it is, unprocessed and clean of any other codes. These can be added for particular investigations. There are two main reasons for this policy.

Firstly, each particular investigation is likely to view the language according to different priorities. Its analytic apparatus may well be valuable and interesting to the next investigator, and even adaptable to the new needs; but not so standardized that it can become an integral part of the corpus.

Secondly, although linguists leap effortlessly to abstractions like 'word' (meaning *lemma*, see Chapter 3) and beyond, they do not all leap in the same way, and they do not devise precise rules for the abstracting. Hence, even the bedrock assumptions of linguistics, like the identification of words, assignment of morphological division, and primary word class, are not at all standardized. Each study helps the others, but does not provide a platform on which the others can directly build.

In the early days of corpus work, the text of other scholars was normally unable to be used by anyone else because there were no standards, and analytic marks were mixed up with the language. Nowadays, we are in danger of having problematic analytical systems imposed on us, derived from traditions of language analysis which have, in the past, specifically rejected corpus evidence. The difficulty arises because those varieties of computational linguistics which used to ignore corpus evidence have quite dramatically switched in recent years in their attitude to corpora, but have retained models of language which are not justified by the evidence they now have.

Basic provision

This conservative approach does not render helpless the corpus manager. A large amount of basic processing is required for the first-stage examination of a text (see Chapter 2), and this can be supplemented by the provision of simple and efficient lemmatizers, taggers, and parsers, which allow deeper investigation during the design of a particular piece of research. If these primary tools are clearly documented, they can sometimes provide short cuts. As far as possible, such facilities should be available on line, rather than done and stored.

Database

The first derived database from a large corpus should be something that cannot be achieved automatically without some intervention from the human researcher. Almost certainly it will be lexically ordered, and almost certainly it will be based on a relational database. To discuss in detail the structure of such databases is outside the scope of this book, but co-ordination of conventions is something to aim for, in Europe, and the world in general. It is becoming urgent in a European context that lexical databases in different languages should be made and kept compatible with each other. The Council of Europe is helping with the co-ordination effort.

Maintenance

Once a corpus is in existence, it needs regular maintenance and upgrading. There are always errors to correct and improvements to be made, adaptations to new hardware and software, and changes in the requirements of users.

In addition, there should be constant attention to the retrieval systems, and processing and analytic tools. For some time to come, software will improve dramatically and frequently.

Different kinds of corpora

Sample corpora

It is about thirty years since the pioneers in this field, Kučera and Francis (1967), set about creating a corpus of major importance, and their foresight continues to be acknowledged as still more investigations commence using the Brown corpus. The more recent work by Johansson (1980) and colleagues, in producing a parallel corpus of British English, adds another dimension of comparison. These corpora have made it possible for research workers to inspect physically texts of greater length than was previously possible (except for some devoted but highly restricted manual counting), and to visualize the further possibilities of using longer texts. Both the information available in Brown and LOB, and the restrictions that their structure imposes, are of benefit to the research. The main structural features of these corpora are:

- a classification into genres (15) of printed text;
- a large number (500) of fairly short extracts (2,000 words), giving a total of around one million words;
- a close to random selection of extracts within genres.

With the dimensions of extracts, and their relationships—fairly regular and known—a great amount of useful information can be extracted with ease from these corpora.

'Ease' is a relative term, and makes light of the decade and more of strenuous work between the preparation of the texts and their exploitation. Now, at least, we can say that the focus of interest has shifted from the manipulation of the information in the corpora to its interpretation. And in some of the more ambitious projects, the limitations of the corpora are beginning to show.

I should like to call corpora of this type *sample corpora*. Brown is a sample of American printed English of the year 1961. Its validity resides in the care taken over its preparation and the clarity of its internal structure. If it is used for an inappropriate purpose, the researcher is forewarned. For example, since the limitation on continuous text is 2,000 words, any study of largish text patterns is likely

23

to be inappropriate. Its vocabulary is controlled only indirectly via the genre classification, so a study of the patterning of infrequent words is doomed, and, indeed, the only words for which it is reliable are those which occur frequently in a good range of genres.

Such a corpus does not purport to be a valid sample of each genre. The overriding consideration is the printed language as a whole, as the standardized package shows. If a million words is hazarded as a reasonable sample of one state of a language, then the sub-categories necessary to balance the sample are not in themselves reasonable samples because they are too brief. No matter what the target size, this point would still be valid. A sample corpus will be discontinuous; its subdivisions will not stand as samples themselves.

The progress of hardware and software development, however, offers opportunities for the analysis of texts of much greater length. Some information, particularly on the patterns of frequent words, can be derived from sample corpora of one million words, but it was clear some years ago that at least another order of magnitude was required to deal with vocabulary. This was achieved in the early eighties (Sinclair, ed., 1988), and it is clear that the user community already requires that yet another order of magnitude is attempted.

The current state of British research is that corpora of up to twenty million words of the contemporary language are available routinely. Of the other languages of Europe, some (for example, German, Italian, Swedish) are in a similar position, and several others are not far behind. In the United States, a project has been launched to gather one billion words very quickly.

Quantities in the spoken language are more modest, but show the same tendency. The first corpus, in 1961, was a mere 135,000 words (Jones and Sinclair 1974), and the spoken element of the Birmingham corpus was 1.5 million in 1985. Moves are now afoot to provide between 10 million and 20 million words of spoken English for the 1990s. In between, the London–Lund corpus of about 350,000 words was made available in a scholarly form in 1980, and this has been the foundation of several studies (Svartvik and Quirk, eds., 1980).

Monitor corpora

This surge in activity and sharp rise in dimension has come about in part because of technological developments. Computer storage is now cheap and vast amounts can be searched by fairly small processors. The linguists' ideal machine, with a small brain and big body, affectionately called a dinosaur a few years ago, is now a reality at many work stations in different parts of the world.

Computer typesetting, not very common ten years ago, is now standard from desk-top publishing to enormous newspaper presses, and word processors and electronic mail pour out billions of words a day in electronic form. If a small proportion of this can be harnessed, there will be no shortage of text, no matter how voracious the computer system.

However, the difference in the up-to-the-minute is one of quality, not quantity. Looking through the computer, the whole state of a language can be passed before one's eyes. There is less need to build up sample corpora slowly and carefully, hoard them, and subject them to intensive examination, when there is no limit to be placed on text length.

It is now possible to create a new kind of corpus, one which has no final extent because, like the language itself, it keeps on developing. Most of the material will come in from machine-readable sources, and it will be examined for the purposes of making routine records. Gradually, it will get too large for any practicable handling, and will be effectively discarded. The focus of attention will be on what information can be gleaned from the text as it passes through a set of filters which will be designed to reflect the concerns of researchers.

We do not need to cherish text; we live in a time of textual explosion. Those texts that have great intrinsic value are not the prime concern of this work, and will be lovingly preserved by other agencies. The study of them will be much enhanced by comparing them with the general picture which the general corpus will provide.

Features of a monitor corpus

So, at any one time, the corpus will have a large and up-to-date selection of current English available; it will have a historical dimension, and it will have a comprehensive word list because of its elaborate record-keeping. Such a corpus is needed at least for every language which has international status.

Sampling can be done according to individual requirements on gigantic, ever-moving stores of text, and detailed evidence of language evolution can be held efficiently.

This new type of corpus I should like to call a *monitor corpus,* because of its capacity to hold a 'state of the language' for research purposes. The information which a sample corpus cannot provide can be retrieved by manipulation of a monitor corpus.

It would be unwise to make light of the difficulties that face the first builders of a monitor corpus. Although the hardware is adequate, the conventions for using its processing power are not geared to this work. Text availability demands the co-operation of major industries in a sensitive area. The achievement of a balanced flow of text is more difficult than in a sample corpus. Efficiency in software will become one of the highest priorities, where until now it has rarely been an issue. More demanding still, the forward vision of those involved will be crucial in determining the long-term value of the work.

Thirty years ago, the possibility of a sample corpus was recognized, and now it is a standard research tool. Now, the possibility of a monitor corpus is clear, and we may expect a lot of activity in the next few years in expanding the horizons of corpus work.

It is reasonable, for English, to aim for a monitor corpus of the language as the next step in research provision: this would be a 'Bank of English' allowing new kinds of access to the patterns of the language which bombard readers every day, but which, because of the circumstances of language use, are inaccessible to direct observation.

2
Basic text processing

Introduction

The basic techniques for processing texts by computer were developed some years ago in the investigation of vocabulary patterns (Jones and Sinclair 1974; Reed 1977). However, they were not readily available to most researchers because they required access to mainframe computers, and often considerable expertise in computing, because early systems were not user-friendly. Also, despite the apparent power of big computers, in practice there have been many problems in achieving ease and reliability in carrying out basic processing, when the text is more than a few thousand words long.

Now computers are much more accessible, both small ones with ever more progressive specifications, and large ones with sophisticated interactive operating systems, and networks of increasing versatility to link them up. Many text stores exist, and it is becoming easier to make them with the rapid growth of information technology. So the opportunity to process long texts is within the grasp of most serious researchers.

It is, therefore, a good moment to review the basic techniques of language data-processing, and to assess their value in linguistic research. At the very least, the quality of linguistic evidence is going to be improved out of all recognition, because of the power of the computer in data management. But it is more than likely that these co-ordinated resources of man and machine will lead to new postulates in theory.

The computer is incurably and pedantically data oriented. For a linguist, there are no short cuts to his or her abstractions. The first stage of adaptation is to resign oneself to plodding through the detail. Attention to detail makes one rapidly aware of oversimplification, and some of the accepted generalizations seem to be in need of a tighter specification. It now seems likely that the relation between data and abstractions, so painfully exposed by the computer, is going to become a major research area.

Input

Once a text has been selected for study, the first decision is in what way it is to be re-created inside the computer. It may seem a simple enough process, to reproduce a text inside the machine, but in practice not all the features of a text are coded. Different features are picked out according to the needs of the work. For most general processing the text is kept to a very simple format—usually a single long string of letters, spaces, and punctuation marks. The letters of the alphabet, punctuation marks, and the word spaces are called *characters*; the distinction between upper and lower case is preserved. Page and line numbers are kept only for reference purposes, and other layout, setting, and type-face information is discarded.

That is all, then, that the computer 'knows' about text—a long succession of nondescript characters marked off in pages and lines.

Words and word-forms

There has been some research based purely on counting the characters, but most students move quickly to some simple notion of a word. The one used here is a *word-form*, and that is an unbroken succession of letters (the hyphen and apostrophe need special attention, but I shall not go into such detail here).

Note that a word-form is close to, but not identical to, the usual idea of a word. In particular, several different word-forms may all be regarded as instances of the same word. So *drive, drives, driving, drove, driven,* and perhaps *driver, drivers, drivers', driver's, drive's,* make up ten different word-forms, all related to the word *drive*. It is usual in defining a word-form to ignore the distinction between upper and lower case, so *SHAPE, Shape,* and *shape,* will all be taken as instances of the same word-form. This convention no doubt blurs a few hundred useful distinctions, like *polish* and *Polish*, but obliterates many thousands of word-forms which have an initial capital letter merely because they begin a sentence. For other purposes this distinction is valuable, but on balance, for studying word-forms, it is best ignored.

There is always a strong temptation to add special editing signs to a text at input. All sorts of jobs would be much easier if, for example, confusable words were kept separate from the start. Two very common English words have each two quite different functions. *To* is both a preposition and the word used to introduce the infinitive form of the verb; it would be very efficient if they were marked *to¹* and *to²* from the start. Similarly, *that* is both a demonstrative and a conjunction. However, if we yield to this temptation, it is clear that special routines will be required to retrieve the original words, and that in general we are distorting the text. Another worker coming unawares upon our text might have great difficulty in deriving accurate information from it.

The computer can find, sort, and count word-forms fairly easily; it finds the conventional notion of a word much more vague and complicated, and there is no standard procedure for converting word-forms to words. For example, should *meanest* and *meaning* be related together, as forms of the word *mean*? There are thousands of such problems, and new research of this kind will rest on better foundations if the greatest use is made of the simplest categories.

Already, it is clear that, in the absence of standardization, the *ad hoc* decisions of one researcher do not suit the next, and much of the laborious work of gathering and presenting basic information has to be done afresh in each project. The best way to keep this wastage to a minimum is to work for as long as possible with data in a form close to its physical occurrence, and only to introduce abstractions where these are unavoidable. Linguistics usually operates with more abstract categories, with words rather than word-forms, because human beings can appreciate that kind of concept; but, in computing, such concepts are indeterminate. Hence, it is good policy to defer the use of them for as long as possible, to refrain from imposing analytical categories from the outside until we have had a chance to look very closely at the physical evidence.

The relationship between word-forms and words is pursued in Chapters 3 and 4.

Text and vocabulary

Using the simple notion of a word-form, we can now represent a text as a succession of word-forms. The word-forms can be counted, so that the length of the text, measured in word-forms, can be calculated. Next, the word-forms can be compared with each other, and it will be found that there are many repetitions of the same word-form. So another count can be made of the number of different word-forms, which is called the *vocabulary* of the text.

In this account, I shall frequently refer to a short sample passage which is printed in Appendix I, at the back of the book. Its length in word-forms is 189. This is often called the number of *running words* in the text. Such a short passage is only of use in illustrating the processes: in actual research, texts are thousands or millions of running words in length. But by using a short text, it is possible for the reader to follow exactly what the computer does, which would be impracticable to explain discursively.

Frequency list—first occurrence

Anyone studying a text is likely to need to know how often each different word-form occurs in it. The simplest operation is to turn it into a list of the word-forms in the order of their first occurrence, noting the frequency of each. Each successive word-form is compared with each previous one. If it is a new word-form it is provided with a counter set at 1; if the word-form has occurred before, it is deleted from the text and 1 is added to the counter at the place of first occurrence of the word-form. For example, if the text is ridiculously short ('The cat sat on the mat'), this operation would give the result:

the 2
cat 1
sat 1
on 1
mat 1

(See Figure 1, in Appendix I, for a longer example taken from the sample text. Note that the sample text and Figures 1–14 are to be found at the back of the book in Appendix I.)

This kind of list is helpful as a quick guide to the way words are distributed in a text, and for a number of more specific purposes. For example, if two word-forms have about the same frequency, but one occurs early in the text and the other does not occur until late, then this difference may alert the student to look for an interpretation. Again, if, in a technical text, there is very little technical vocabulary for some time and then a rush of it, that may be a clue to a high-level structural boundary in the text, perhaps the end of a general, layman's introduction to a technical subject. Figure 1, in Appendix I, shows how *human* and *language* open up a new topic in the sample text.

Such observations can help a lot in the selection of texts for English teaching. At present, selections are made on an intuitive basis, and there is no guarantee that a fragment of text is representative of the book or paper it came from. Quite often, what appears to be introductory matter is offered as typical technical text.

A frequency list of word-forms is never more than a set of hints or clues to the nature of a text. By examining a list, one can get an idea of what further information would be worth acquiring: or one can make guesses about the structure of the text, and so focus an investigation.

This kind of information—about the clustering of vocabulary in various patterns in long texts—has been studied in detail by Martin Phillips (1985 *et seq.*).

Frequency list—alphabetical

The information that is now available in the frequency list can be rendered in several ways. The most common are **a.** alphabetical order (Figure 2) and **b.** frequency order (Figure 3). Both these lists can, of course, be placed in ascending or descending order. In Figure 3, word-forms of the same frequency are arranged alphabetically.

The main use of alphabetical lists is for reference, but they are occasionally useful as objects of study. They are often helpful in formulating hypotheses to be tested, and checking assumptions that have been made. For example, where rough estimates are to be made, they are sometimes used (for example, in Kjellmer 1984, which uses the reverse order lists of Brown 1963). Mostly, however, alphabetical lists play a secondary role, available when there is a need to check the frequency of a particular word-form.

Frequency list—frequency order

The same information can be sorted again so that the list begins with the most frequent item, and continues down to the single occurrences (see Figure 3). In a text of a thousand words or more, this is a document worth studying—in a short text, of course, the reasons for word-frequency are too local to be very interesting.

The listing for a particular text can be compared to that of other texts or to large collections of language. The most frequent items tend to keep a stable distribution, and so any marked change in their order can be significant. Figure 4 shows the top of a frequency list of about eighteen million words.

Word frequency profiles

The examination of frequency lists can be aided by simple statistical information such as provided in Figures 5 and 6. To explain these, let us examine line 3 in Figure 5. This line deals with word-forms which occur three times. Column 2 tells us that there are four of them, and column 3 keeps a running total of the number of different word-forms that have been reported. Column 4 relates the number in column 3 with the total of 113, expressed as a percentage. So the word-forms that occur no more than three times constitute 92.04 per cent of the 'vocabulary'—the number of different word-forms.

Column 5 considers the running text, where the total number of word-forms is 189. If there are four word-forms which occur three times each, then 12 must be added to the previous total in column 5. Column 6 relates the number in column 5 to the total of 189 and reports that word-forms that occur no more than three times occupy 67.2 per cent of the text. This figure will drop as the text size increases. In longer texts, the most frequent word-form, *the*, itself occupies about 2.5 per cent of the text.

Figure 6 is similar to Figure 5, but presents the information the other way round. If we follow the line beginning with 3 again, column 2 is the same, but column 3 gives a total, out of 113, of the number of different word-forms with a frequency of 3 or more. Column 4 reports this as only 11.5 per cent of the total. Column 5 shows that these more frequent words account for 74 word-forms in the text, and column 6 points out that 74 is 39.15 per cent of the total of 189 separate word-forms in the text.

Concordances

The computer presents us with co-occurrence information in the basic form of a concordance. A *concordance* is a collection of the occurrences of a word-form, each in its own textual environment. In its simplest form, it is an index. Each word-form is indexed, and a reference is given to the place of each occurrence in a text. Figure 7 is an example of this type.

KWIC (Key Word in Context)

For many years now the KWIC format has been widely used in data-processing; it saves the researcher looking up each occurrence. The word-form under examination appears in the centre of each line, with extra space on either side of it. The length of the context is specified for different purposes. Here is a concordance to 'The cat sat on the mat' with just one word-form printed on either side (+1). The central words are in alphabetical order:

the	cat	sat
the	mat	
sat	on	the
cat	sat	on
	the	cat
on	the	mat

Figure 8 shows a concordance to the word-form *is* in the sample text, with four word-forms printed on either side (± 4).

The full KWIC format prints a whole line of text, with the word under examination in the middle.

Longer environments

Figure 8 shows an environment of four word-forms on either side of the word-form in the centre. This pattern can be varied according to need, though the visual convenience is lost if the citation exceeds one line. Figure 9 shows the same concordance for *is*, but with an environment of a whole sentence in each case. The computer can be asked to provide according to many different specifications, and evidently it is found to be most convenient to make concordances as and when they are required. As a word or phrase is studied, it may become clear that additional context is needed.

Ordering within concordances

The basic concordance at Figure 8 lists occurrences in text order, just as the basic word list is in order of occurrence. However, within the concordance to a particular word-form, it is easy to arrange for other orderings. The one which has been found most generally helpful is alphabetical ordering to the right of the central word-form (see Figure 10). This ordering highlights phrases and other patterns that begin with the central word. For example, in the short sample text in Appendix I, the word-form *only* shows up immediately to the right of the central word *is*.

33

Another presentation of interest is reverse alphabetization to the left of the central form (see Figure 11). This points up the occurrence of *it* and *the activity* to the left of the central word *is*. *The activity* refers to *communication*, and *it* refers to *human verbal communication*, which is stated to be a small subsection of communication. This is a useful clue to the topic of the passage, in that four of the cited clauses have such a similar subject. Closer examination shows that two other examples— lines 1 and 4—also have subjects centring on communication; that all the others, except line 9, show another type of subject; and that line 9 (*boast*) is different again, and on its own.

From this brief example, it can be seen how, with appropriate systems of analysis and reference, a computer-supported investigation can be, quick, efficient, and useful.

Concordance processing

It is valuable to think of a concordance as a text in itself, and to examine the frequencies of word-forms in the environment of the central word-form. Some very common words (for example, *the, and, of*) will show a frequency that is much the same as their overall frequency in the language, but others will show a strong influence from being close to the central word-form in the concordance.

An alphabetical list and a frequency list of the concordance at Figure 8 have been prepared in Figure 12 and Figure 13, as if Figure 8 were an ordinary text. (Note that where two occurrences of *is* are close together, the same text word-form can occur more than once in the environment and so its frequency in the concordance can be greater than its frequency in the original text. So *active, highly, small,* and *subsection,* occur once only in the text, but twice within four words of an occurrence of *is*.)

In such a short text, we cannot expect the linguistically-important patterns to be distinguishable from all the other statistical effects of the process. The word-form *is*, in any case, is unlikely to have strong lexical collocations of a conventional nature. But the method is clear from these examples.

Text analysis statistics

As soon as the computer has been trained to identify characters, word-forms, and sentences, it can produce figures for a number of relation-

34

ships—see Figure 14. This can be very useful in comparing texts, or searching for texts with particular characteristics.

Selective information

When a text is very long, the word lists will also be long, and the concordances will be extremely long. Not all this information is needed every time, hence it is important to be able to select. Selections can be made as follows:

a. By frequency. If we omit from a frequency list word-forms which only occur once, it shrinks to about half its size. Also, for some purposes we only require a list of very frequent words (for example, Figure 4). It is commonplace to distinguish roughly between grammatical and lexical items by this means. At other times, it is useful to divide the vocabulary of a text into frequency bands.

b. By form. It is possible to specify words by their alphabetical make-up, or by the letters in them, or by a combination of both, like 'three-letter words beginning with t'. It will be found that specifications like these can be devised which allow a researcher to pick out several word-classes, for example, present participles, or regular adverbs.

These two types of selection can also be combined to make sensitive analytical instruments, at least for pilot study.

Intermediate categories

When a researcher has easy access to the processing described so far, it is possible to formulate objectives in linguistic description, and devise procedures for pursuing these objectives. A considerable amount of research on specific topics can be launched—in stylistics, for example, and in English language teaching. In cases where rather simple categories like word-form are adequate, there is no need to pursue more abstract categories, and indeed good reason not to.

For many purposes, however, and for research into language structure in general, it is desirable to establish intermediate categories like *word*; word-classes like *adverb, adjective*; larger syntactic categories like *phrase, clause*, and *lexical item* (units comprising one or more morphemes). (See, for example, Yang 1986.)

The specification of categories of this kind is a purely practical matter; the researcher has to devise a selection procedure which matches his or her intuition, and is consistent with authoritative published descriptions. In all probability, there will be some tentative rules, formulated in terms of the physical data, to capture surface regularities. These will need to be amended by removing irrelevancies and rectifying omissions. Even then, it must be recognized that the procedure will be prone to a small measure of discrepancy.

The discrepancies between the way a computer can identify things in a text and the expectations of a person who knows the language of the text is well worth investigation. In Computer Assisted Language Learning (CALL), this kind of discrepancy can be used to make students aware of the exact rules of, for example, morphology. In automatic analysis (see Garside *et al.* 1987), it is the central problem for automatic parsing. Similar problems have dampened enthusiasm for machine translation.

New approaches

The most exciting aspect of long-text data-processing, however, is not the mirroring of intuitive categories of description. It is the possibility of new approaches, new kinds of evidence, and new kinds of description. Here, the objectivity and surface validity of computer techniques become an asset rather than a liability. Without relinquishing our intuitions, of course, we try to find explanations that fit the evidence, rather than adjusting the evidence to fit a pre-set explanation.

It is clear that the early stages of computer processing give results which conflict with our intuitions. In addition to problems in identifying word-classes, the notion of collocation turns out to be not nearly as simple as it looks. Current work in lexicography shows that, for many common words, the most frequent meaning is not the one that first comes to mind and takes pride of place in most dictionaries.

Progress will be made by trying to relate these conflicting positions. No one would wish to give priority to either at the expense of the other. The computer is not a device which will produce sensible categories without guidance, but, on the other hand, a linguistic description which is not supported by the evidence of the language has no credibility.

New evidence from long texts, where the computer does little more than clerical work, is challenging our current linguistic descriptions quite fundamentally. Such evidence has not been available before, and its assimilation should contribute to the maturation of linguistics as a discipline.

3
The evidence of usage

Introduction

When a corpus is available, and tools for basic processing are available, it is possible to examine the evidence and compare the computer's view with other kinds of evidence. In this chapter, we concentrate on dictionaries, but the principles are the same for grammatical evidence.

The main sources of lexicographic evidence are, probably in order of popularity:

1 other dictionaries;
2 users' ideas about their language;
3 observation of language in use.

These three types of evidence are roughly the same as would be invoked for any enterprise in language description:

1 existing descriptions of the language;
2 native-speaker introspections;
3 text, i.e. language in use.

Existing descriptions

The great value of existing descriptions is that the information is already organized. Language change is not so rapid that descriptions go out of date quickly, and even over decades we tend to assume that most existing work is valid and accurate. A synthesis of good practice, with obvious corrections and updatings, should produce a reliable dictionary fairly quickly.

However, there are disadvantages to relying upon existing lexicography:

a. It is difficult to know when a word or a usage lapses; hence, for a contemporary record, the evidence of existing dictionaries is misleading.

37

b. Mistakes in the organization of an entry are difficult to detect, since they only become noticeable when compiling starts from scratch.

c. New developments in linguistic description, for example pragmatic information, cannot easily be fitted into established lexicographic formats or indeed into the whole conceptual background of lexicography. Received information cannot be shaken free of its theoretical origins.

Where good evidence is available from other sources, existing dictionaries are very helpful as a check on coverage, because the bigger ones are repositories of a very large amount of information. As a general rule, though, a form or a meaning should not be incorporated in a new compilation unless it is independently confirmed. The operation of this rule would gradually rid dictionaries of two types of red herring:

a. Forms and/or meanings which have lapsed into disuse, but are not so indicated. For a contemporary dictionary, this leaves space for newcomers or for further information about the modern language; for a historical dictionary, it will help the dating of language change, to record both when a meaning comes into the language and when it drops out.

b. Forms and/or meanings which are constructs of lexicography, and which do not really exist, in the sense that there is no textual evidence for them. The line between what is possible and what is reasonably natural is not easy to draw, and it would constitute a diversion here to explore it in any detail (see Sinclair 1984). But lexicographers should be scrupulous in extirpating these items.

The tradition of historical dictionaries has led to some ideas of a dictionary as an archive of usages which once were, but are no longer, or a museum of rare and unusual language events. Once in, no word or phrase need ever hope to leave. Another view of a dictionary—one suited to the concept of a dictionary of the contemporary language—is that the omission of a word is just as significant as its inclusion. A dictionary of this type will not support archaic usage and will warn about rare and specialized uses.

No one likes to look up a word in a dictionary and find it is not there, so there will always be room for the historical dictionary, to cope with a tiny margin of uncharacteristic usage. However, dictionaries are being used more and more to guide production and composition, and this is where the user needs a dictionary whose information is known to be up to date. The words in such a dictionary are words which can be safely used, in the meanings and contexts that are indicated.

Native-speaker introspections

These can be subdivided into:

a. informant testing—for example, reports by users on their usage;
b. introspection by the linguist.

Informant testing, whether formal or informal, produces some useful evidence. The informal type is very common and usually gives rise to lively, if rarely resolved discussion. More formal investigation is limited because of the time it takes, and needs to be carefully prepared and conducted. It is unlikely to become a major source of lexicographic evidence.

The special case of the lexicographer being his or her own informant is worth special consideration. It has been fashionable among grammarians for many years now to introspect and to trust their intuitions about structure; why should not vocabulary be investigated in the same way?

The problem about all kinds of introspection is that it does not give evidence about usage. The informant will not be able to distinguish among various kinds of language patterning—psychological associations, semantic groupings, and so on. Actual usage plays a very minor role in one's consciousness of language and one would be recording largely ideas about language rather than facts of it. Ultimately, however, the lexicographic decisions will be personal evaluations by the lexicographer, giving due consideration to all the evidence that he or she has amassed. Personal introspection will inevitably play a big part at that point, being inextricable from all the other points that bear on a decision. This seems to be the most favourable point for the operation of introspection—in evaluating evidence rather than creating it.

Language in use

I have thus suggested that both the evidence of secondary sources and the evidence of introspection should be brought in at a late stage in the process of compilation. It follows that the initial evidence should always be of the third type—from the observation of language in use.

Here again, I would like make a distinction between two sub-types:

a. citation of instances;
b. concordancing of texts.

The first sub-type is the cornerstone of traditional lexicography. Citations, frequently from authoritative sources, formed the basis of Dr Johnson's evidence, and established a central principle in lexicography. The *Oxford English Dictionary (OED)* 'worked a revolution in the art of lexicography' by having as its basis 'a collection of some five millions of excerpts from English literature'. This 'collection of evidence ... represented by a selection of about 1,800,000 quotations actually printed—could form the only possible foundation for ... the work' (Preface to the *OED* 1933).

The Historical Introduction to the *OED* speaks with feeling about both the importance and the capriciousness of the evidence thus gathered by citation of instances: 'Johnson and Richardson had been selective in the material they assembled, and obviously some kind of selection would be imposed by practical limits, however wide the actual range might be. This was a point on which control was difficult; the one safeguard was that the care and judgement of some readers would make up for the possible deficiencies of others.'

At the time when the *OED* was being planned and produced, the gathering of individual instances selected by a wide variety of voluntary readers was probably the best available method of amassing evidence, and for any dictionary with the historical scope of the *OED* it may still be necessary to use this method in part, despite its unreliability. However, for most lexicographic purposes, it is now possible to use the organizing power of modern computers to establish new principles and standards in the gathering of citational evidence. This is type **b.** above—the complete concordancing of a representative corpus of texts.

The selection process becomes a selection of texts for the corpus, not instances for a dictionary. Once it is decided to include a text, then all the instances of all the words constitute the evidence.

The technique of creating a corpus for linguistic study is outlined in Chapter 1. The criteria tend towards the sociolinguistic. A clear account of the selection criteria and procedures for the Brown corpus of one million words, paralleled by the LOB corpus, can be found in Hofland and Johannson (1982), and for the Birmingham Collection of English Texts, in Renouf (1987). More specialized corpora on various principles are at different stages of planning and creation, and one can confidently predict a period of great activity in this field, fuelling the lexicography of the 1990s and beyond.

Word-forms and lemmas

Given a corpus in machine-readable form, the next stage is to derive some basic information from it. The simplest computer access to a text is to regard it as a linear string of characters. Each character corresponds to a key on the keyboard, so the word-space character can be used to define a word, rather crudely, and the words so defined can be counted and arranged in various ways. At this stage, a 'word' is any string of characters with a word space on either side, so *boy* and *boys*, and *come*, *comes*, *came* are all different words.

There is a lot to be learnt about a language from the study of it in this simple format. Most studies leap ahead and group the crude words according to simple notions of meaning, instead of deriving as much information as possible from each stage in the developing sophistication of description. This crude notion of a basic linguistic unit I have called (in Chapter 2) a word-form; it is one of the absolutes in the written language—a string of letters with a space on either side.

When we talk of 'the word *come*', meaning *come* or *comes* or *coming* or *came*, I should like to use the word *lemma*. So the initial statement often found in dictionaries, for example:

come /kʌm/ vb comes, com + ing, came, come

is an expression of the relationship between the lemma and its forms.

Chapter 2 shows how information about the word-forms can be prepared. This information can then be related to the lemmas; but problems begin to arise, since a lemma is not obvious to a computer.

The machine can simply be painstakingly told, lemma by lemma, how each lemma relates to the word-forms in the texts. Or some automatic routine can be devised which should, with reasonable accuracy, group the forms into lemmas, and, most importantly, should present any problem cases to the researcher.

Lemmatization looks fairly straightforward, but is actually a matter of subjective judgement by the researcher. There are thousands of decisions to be taken. Also, it is not yet understood how meanings are distributed among forms of a lemma, and a new branch of study is looming—the interrelationships of a lemma and its forms.

41

This is a valuable study for lexicographers, because there is a close similarity between a lemma, and a *headword* and its inflected and derived forms, in a dictionary. The question of homographs becomes interesting, for example, if one abandons etymological arguments. If two words, historically distinct, have fallen together so that there is just no physical distinction between them, what contemporary arguments can be used for separating them? How many words written *bow* are there in English? The *OED* lists seven headwords; *Webster's New Collegiate* gives five; *Collins English Dictionary* has three; and *Collins COBUILD English Language Dictionary* gives just one. They are all describing the same language facts.

For grammarians, the study of morphology used to be central; and although most work is now done on higher structures, it rests ultimately on the accuracy of the lemmatization. Another interesting question in this area is how to decide what the physical form of a lemma should be. Traditionally, the 'base', or uninflected, form is used even when that form is hardly ever found on its own, or hardly ever found at all. But a case could be made for any of a number of alternatives, for example, that the most frequently-encountered form should be used for the lemma; and the first-stage evidence from the computer can provide a good basis for planning new methods of access to the word-forms of the language.

Concordances

After sorting out the lemmas, we turn to the *concordances*. To begin with, it is easier to use concordances where citations of a word-form are listed. Citations of lemmas are also available, but they are more difficult to study until something is known about the individual word-forms.

The quality of evidence about the language which can be provided by concordances is quite superior to any other method; automatic concordancing of texts has been an established facility for many years now, and for some special studies manual or automatic concordances (for example, to the Bible or Shakespeare) have been used. The early efforts concentrated on established literature, so that quotations and allusions could be located, and figures of speech could be studied; there was no interest in sampling the everyday language. The labour of producing the concordances was so great until recently that only the finest and most complex texts could be prepared for study in this way.

Let us consider some of the factors affecting the shape and utility of concordances:

1 Whether the concordance is selective or exhaustive. The ability to be exhaustive is one of the principal features of a concordance, because it can claim to present all the available information, and is clearly superior to a list of selective citations where there are no strict rules about selection. But there will be circumstances where some selection has to be made, and the principles of selection will be of the greatest importance. At present, the only need for selection is in the case of the very commonest words in very long texts. The pattern of word-occurrence in texts means that for any reasonably long text, there are some words that occur too often, and some that do not occur often enough for their behaviour to be comfortably studied. Consequently, there is only a central set of words for which the evidence is both comprehensive and convenient. So the question of selection of citations can be resolved by two principles:

a. selection is only made when the number of instances becomes quite unmanageable otherwise;
b. the criteria for selection must be very carefully chosen.

2 The length of the citation. The almost universal format for concordances is the KWIC (Key Word in Context—see Chapter 2), where the length of the citation is determined by the width of a bale of computer paper; the key word is in the middle. This format is fairly useful, but for the study of some words, it is not adequate, and other formats must be devised. The length of a citation could be counted by character (as in KWIC), or by word, or by finding punctuation marks to identify sentences—or by a whole range of more sophisticated linguistic criteria. At the present time, the range of concordance formats is growing. Quite often, it is helpful to start off with a simple KWIC concordance and then to switch to a longer context or a sentence context for closer study.

3 Ordering of citations. Where there are tens, hundreds, or thousands of citations of a word-form it is useful to consider how they may be listed for further study. The simplest method is text order, but for some purposes a listing in alphabetical order of the word following the key word can be helpful, and for other purposes an ordering by the preceding word can be helpful, and sometimes both. Whichever method is chosen highlights some patterns for the eye, and obscures others. (See Appendix I, Figures 8–11, for some examples of concordances.)

To improve efficiency, we need criteria for evaluating citations (see Chapter 6), closely followed by criteria for estimating the optimum length of a given citation.

Concordance evidence: an example

Here is a brief example of the kind of evidence that an exhaustive concordance provides; the word chosen is *decline* and its associated forms *declension, declined, declines, declining*. Their occurrence in a general corpus of 7.3 million words is:

decline	122
declined	76
declining	38
declines	9
declension	0
TOTAL	245

Observations from the corpus will be compared with the treatment afforded to the words in the *Collins English Dictionary* (*CED*). (I have chosen the *CED* not as a suitable target for criticism, but because I think it is the most reliable example of current lexicography in its field.)

The *CED* gives an entry for *declension* with three distinct meanings, and a number of other forms which are not in the corpus; some of them seem unlikely starters for any corpus:

Headwords	Derived forms
declinate	declinable
declination	decliner
declinometer	declensional
	declensionally
	declinational

A word must occur to remain in the language, and therefore to be the concern of lexicographers of the contemporary language. So a word which does not occur at all in over seven million words of general current English does not have a strong claim to be prominent in a description, as compared with other words. But we must not, at present, be too rigidly guided by occurrence and frequency statistics. We should always remember that even the multi-million word samples are tiny compared to the amount of language produced in even a smallish community; so an occurrence of zero or close to zero may be just a quirk of the sampling. A description of a language which aims to be comprehensive will have to scan hundreds of millions of words (see 'Monitor corpora' in Chapter 1).

The problem for the lexicographer is that word-formation rules are highly productive, and only the evidence of text is likely to control what is otherwise a monstrous list of forms. If they occurred, they would probably follow the rules of formation, but we know nothing about their behaviour.

Research will, in due course, offer guide-lines which will gradually improve the choice of texts, sampling methods, processing of evidence, and application of the results to lexicography. Until then, we must use the evidence with care; but we must use it.

Words like *declension* and *declinate* may follow a different pattern associated with technical language (Roe 1977; Phillips 1983). Many words and phrases are rare in a general sample of texts but very frequent indeed in certain specific texts. Most vocabulary gives indications of this trend but technical language shows it in an extreme form; presumably *declension* is a fairly common word in a Latin grammar.

The full entry for *decline* in the *CED* is given in Figure 5 below. The *CED* offers two word classes: **vb.** for senses 1–5, and **n.** for 6–9. The sequence 'verb followed by noun' is a significant editorial decision (see the *CED*, page xv), and contrasts, for example, with the treatment of *deck* and *decoy*. These are nearby words that are treated in the order **n.** and then **vb.**

From the concordances, we can glean the following distribution, confining the decision to **vb.** and **n.**:

vb.	n.	TOTAL
136	109	245

Figure 1

Verbal use predominates. Let us now break down the figures for each separate form:

		verb	noun
decline		14	108
declined		76	0
declining		38	0
declines		8	1
TOTAL	245	136	109

Figure 2

The uninflected form, which appears in a dictionary as a headword, does not follow the pattern of the others, but overwhelmingly is used as a noun.

We must also note that the classification of *declining* as verbal is a misleading convention; twenty-six of its occurrences are as noun modifier, closest in syntax to the word class adjective. If this point is reflected in the word-class analysis, the picture changes:

	verbal	nominal	adjectival
decline	14	108	0
declined	76	0	0
declining	38	0	26
declines	8	1	0
TOTAL 245	136	109	26

Figure 3

The different proportions of verb and noun evaporate.

At this point, before we consider the division into senses, we can associate the form *decline* with nominal usage, *declining* with adjectival usage, and *declines*, *declined*, with verbal usage. The proportions of total usage of each form are given in Figure 4:

	verbal	nominal	adjectival	Total
decline	0.12	0.88		1.00
declined	1.00			1.00
declining	0.33		0.67	1.00
declines	0.89	0.11		1.00
TOTAL	0.46	0.44	0.10	1.00

Figure 4

Consider the *CED* entry for *decline*, in Figure 5:

de+cline (dɪˈklaɪn) *vb.* **1.** to refuse to do or accept (something), esp. politely. **2.** (*intr.*) to grow smaller; diminish: *demand has declined over the years.* **3.** to slope or cause to slope downwards. **4.** (*intr.*) to deteriorate gradually, as in quality, health, or character. **5.** *Grammar*, to state or list the inflections of (a noun, adjective, or pronoun), or (of a noun, adjective, or pronoun) to be inflected for number, case, or gender. Compare **conjugate** (sense 1). ~*n.* **6.** gradual deterioration or loss. **7.** a movement downward or towards something smaller; diminution. **8.** a downward slope; declivity. **9.** *Archaic.* any slowly progressive disease, such as tuberculosis. [C14: from Old French

46

decliner to inflect, turn away, sink, from Latin *dēclīnāre* to bend away, inflect grammatically] —de+'clin+a·ble *adj.*—de+'clin+er *n.*

Figure 5: CED entry for **decline**

Of the five verbal senses in the *CED*, numbers 3 (slope gradually) and 5 (grammar) can be discarded, because they do not occur in this data. Senses 2 and 4 are very hard to separate, and only sense 1 stands out.

Sense 1: *to refuse*

We shall continue with some observations on sense 1 (to refuse); note that there is no corresponding nominal sense in the corpus.

Although there are only fourteen instances of the base form used as a verb, they are worth looking at individually because the base form:

a. is used for the present tense, and so can refer to the moment of speaking;
b. can take all pronouns as a subject except *he, she, it*;
c. is used as the imperative form.

Eight of the fourteen instances are of sense 1. Of these, one illustrates clearly what Austin (1962) called a *performative* use. The occurrence of the sentence actually performs the act named by the verb. In *saying* 'I decline ...' you *decline*, for example:

I decline to fuse with Tammy Hall ...

Many English verbs, by their meaning, could have performative uses, but by no means all are used as such; *insult* is an example. Others are not used directly, but only through modal verbs, etc. For example, 'I'll have to charge you £3' could be performative, whereas, 'I charge £3 for this job' is a report, not the verbal presentation of a bill.

There appear to be no such restraints on *decline*, though further instances would be helpful.

The distribution of sense 1 over all the forms of *decline* as verb is as follows:

	Sense 1	Total occurrence as verb	Total occurrences
decline	8	14	122
declined	36	76	76
declining	3	12	38
declines	1	8	9
TOTAL	48	110	245

Figure 6

From this it is clear that only the form *declined* supports sense 1. We shall look further into the pattern of *declined*.

Sense 1 is distinguishable from the others on syntactic grounds. The *-ed* form has several syntactic roles, but in the pattern of *declined* we only need to pursue two of these:

a. the simple past tense—fifty instances;
b. following *have,* etc. to make a perfect verb tense—twenty-three instances.

There are two instances of the word functioning as a non-finite verb in a clause (Appendix II (A) line 28; Appendix II (B) line 8), one of them in a title (Appendix II (B) line 8); there is one instance of *declined* as a noun modifier (Appendix II (B) line 17); and there is nothing else. Specifically, there are two important roles which are not instanced at all:

c. following *be,* etc. to make the passive;
d. clause complement.

Sense 1 is almost confined to occurrence as the simple past tense; there are only three cases where it is preceded by an auxiliary, whereas half of the remaining occurrences are of that type.

In clause structure, sense 1 can occur in transitive structures— hence, one might have expected one or two passives. Of the thirty-six instances only twelve are in transitive structures (including clauses acting as objects). They are listed and numbered in Appendix II (A). Fifteen are followed by an infinitive clause, for example, *to do so* (number 24), which expresses what was declined, and count almost as the equivalent of transitivity in information terms. This leaves nine intransitives, which merit a further glance.

The limitations of this particular concordance format become apparent at this point, whereas in the basic analysis of meaning they have rarely been a frustration. But now we are concerned with textual reference, and may need a longer citation to confirm a hypothesis.

The hypothesis is that whatever is reported as having been declined has already been named, mentioned, or indicated with sufficient clarity; so that the reader, arriving at the word *declined,* need be in no doubt about what would be a suitable object or infinitive clause. The shared knowledge of a community of speakers will normally lead to an understanding of what things can be declined. In number 6, the pronoun *one* refers back to a relevant noun phrase; and in numbers 12 and 18, there are prior clauses which mention what is declined (number 12: *if he would not dance for us*; number 18: *wished to see me urgently*). In number 19, there is *it* the subject of the next clause, which continues a chain of cohesion.

In the other four cases, we just have to guess at what was declined, but that indeterminacy is not a serious flaw. The crucial point is to reach agreement that in each instance there is evidence that what is declined will be found earlier in the text.

If I can assume such agreement, then all the instances of the first meaning are 'text-transitive'. Whatever is declined is expressed in the text in one way or another. This improves on the classic indecision of dictionaries about transitivity, enshrined in the meaningless message **v.t. + i.**, and discreetly suppressed to **vb.** in the *CED*.

Other senses
The *CED* leaves us with two verbal senses which echo nominal ones:

2. to grow smaller; diminish (*compare* 7. a movement downward or towards something smaller; diminution)
4. to deteriorate gradually, as in quality, health, or character (*compare* 6. gradual deterioration or loss).

Sense 7 expresses the difficulty of separating these senses:

a. they are rather close together, concerning reductions in quantity and quality. In the *CED*, sense 2 quotes *diminish* whose own entry in turn quotes *depreciate*;
b. those instances which are pretty clearly of sense 2/7, nevertheless carry a strong shading of sense 4/6.

The pattern is a small-scale example of the indeterminacy of categorization which is brought out in Stock (1984). My tentative assignments are set out in Figure 7, which excludes the forty-eight instances of sense 1, but the overwhelming impression is that categorization here is an artificial exercise. Appendix II (B) contains all the instances of *declined* except for those which are clearly sense 1.

	mainly sense 2/7	medial or doubtful	mainly sense 4/6	Total
NOUN USES	21	18	70	109
decline	20	18	70	108
declines	1			1
VERB USES	36	14	12	62
decline	3	1	2	6
declined	24	9	7	40
declines	3	3	1	7
declining	6	1	2	9
ADJECTIVE USES	15	4	7	26
(declining)				
TOTAL	72	36	89	197

Figure 7

There is a small amount of structural evidence to distinguish these senses in the case of *decline* (noun). It tends towards the 'deterioration' sense when there is no qualifying phrase in the noun group, and where the qualifier is an *of* phrase. The 'deterioration' sense is likely when there is a possessive modifier, and in the phrase *in decline*. On the other hand, a qualifier which is an *in* phrase usually signals the sense of size reduction.

These structural points are not matched by anything in the verbal uses, where all the gradations between the two senses can be found. In one example, where they are yoked together, there is no suggestion of a pun on the verb meaning.

The RCP declined in spirit and in numbers ... (Appendix II (B) line 33)

Collocational evidence often supports the sense of reduction in size with numerals, *per, average; population, economic profitability; gradual, sharp, slowly*. The sense of deterioration is supported by, for example, *sad, quality, Britain, commitment, suffered*. Strangely, perhaps, the word *rapid* is associated with this sense.

The result of this study is that there are no sharp boundaries within a fairly broad sense area. Most examples are a blend of the two main senses, and many are not at all clear on the constitution of the blend.

From this brief example, we can make suggestions for how *decline* should be handled in a dictionary or a grammar. If we assume that the primary categorization in a dictionary should be by sense, then there is only one major distinction in sense, between the 'refuse' sense and the 'reduce' one. The slight indications of an earlier sense of 'slope' might be mentioned or ignored according to the policy of the dictionary.

With respect to the 'reduce' continuum it would be important to note that on the whole, nominal usage tends towards 'deteriorate', while verbal and adjectival use shows the opposite inclination. The form *decline* is heavily nominal, *declining* adjectival, *declined* verbal. Instances which carry little or no trace of the 'deteriorate' sense are of a slightly technical nature—economic journalism and the like.

The other main sense, of 'refuse', is verbal, associated particularly with *declined*. Syntactically it is text-transitive, and pragmatically it is performative. Hence the grammar will use the same basic categorization as the dictionary.

The general conclusion is that much greater precision can be gained in language work by studying instances which are gathered objectively. We select texts and then consider all the instances. It also appears that grammatical and lexical distinctions may be closer together than is normally allowed.

4
Sense and structure in lexis

Introduction

In the last chapter, we ended up with a simple correlation between the two main meanings of a word and the two main choices in verb transitivity. It raised the prospect that there is a close correlation between the different senses of a word and the structures in which it occurs. 'Structures' includes lexical structure in terms of collocations and similar patterns. 'Senses of a word' includes the contribution that a word may make to a multi-word lexical item.

This chapter investigates such a hypothesis more closely, by looking at an apparently much more difficult case, that of the lemma *yield*. The choice of *yield* is not random, but neither is it chosen because it supports the hypothesis.

One criterion for the selection of this lemma was that the total number of occurrences would not be overwhelming for presentational purposes, and another was that both technical and non-technical (and, if possible, sub-technical) senses would be exemplified. Initially, just the form *yield* was studied, but the other forms of the lemma, *yielded*, *yielding*, and *yields* were added later. The question is how close is the correlation; how regular and how important is the hypothesis of a close correlation between sense and structure—if substantiated—in linguistic description?

The selection of *yield* was made for purposes quite distinct from investigation of this hypothesis, and the sense–structure correlation shown by this lemma only emerged in detailed analysis. So it is reasonably likely that the sort of patterns shown below are to be found in other words, and this surmise is supported by the many informal and partial observations which led to the formulation of the hypothesis in the first instance.

Evidence: main senses

For this study, I used the central corpus of the Birmingham Collection of English Texts. This is approximately 7.3 million words in length, built up from a representative set of texts in contemporary written and spoken English (see Renouf 1984). In this collection, there are 125 instances of the lemma *yield* as follows:

yield   51
yielded   25
yielding 20
yields   29

A concordance listing of these 125 occurrences in KWIC format alphabetized to the right of the central word is given in Appendix III (which is to be found at the back of the book). This number of instances should be enough to outline the meaning and use of a word, but the results can always be checked with reference to the total corpus holdings. In the quoted examples in this chapter, incomplete words at the beginnings and ends of lines are suppressed.

There is a prominent meaning of *yield* which we can gloss as 'give way'. A typical dictionary definition (from *Collins English Dictionary* (CED)) is:

To give way, submit or surrender, as through force or persuasion.

In the concordance, all four forms of *yield* occur in this meaning. Here are some clear examples (followed by their order-of-listing number in the concordance):

... But we did not yield then and we shall not yield now. On the wall of his office, Professor ... (24)

Watergate conversation, which Mr Nixon agreed to yield to the courts, 'did not exist'. As it ... (35)

... modernise their precepts of Judaic orthodoxy, and yield to the demands of Western culture as well as ... (42)

... means to prevent it. Ovid recommends: 'Love yields to business, be employed, you're safe, and ... (122)

... as once the masculine province of the area but is yielding and its glamour has been somewhat ... (84)

... to Denmark and Sweden. In Sweden the authorities yielded at once to the threats which swiftly ... (56)

There is another prominent meaning of *yield* which we can gloss as 'produce', though the meaning is restricted to production by a prearranged process. It is often found in technical usage (though the corpus contains no really specialized material). A typical definition is:

> ... to give forth or supply, esp. by cultivation, labour, etc. ... to furnish as a return (*CED* 1979)

In the concordance, the form *yields* is prominently associated with this meaning. Here are some examples of *yield* and *yields*, occurring as nouns:

> ... that could fire a nuclear shell with a 15 kiloton yield about the same size bomb which destroyed ... (1)
>
> ... the water 100 per cent and have a far better yield than any farm round here for miles. Our ... (32)
>
> ... more fertilizer than Europe to achieve similar yields. In 1975, developed countries used an ... (99)
>
> ... acute proportions. At Bangladesh's low average yields of half a ton of rice per acre, a man ... (118)

There is a third important meaning of *yield* which is less easy to pin down, since it appears to be a weak extension of the 'produce' meaning. It does not actually have a very strong meaning, and so it does not contrast sharply with the others. It can be glossed as 'leads to', or 'provides'. Here are some clear examples:

> ... the interaction of these different approaches to yield an effective answer. (11)
>
> ... adolescents. Free acting out and talking through yields satisfaction. At the same time it ... (119)
>
> ... inevitable. In the meantime, dolphin research is yielding new data on the ways in which man's ... (88)
>
> ... or Germans - detente was not a useless exercise. It yielded positive results, defusing the troubling ... (64)

Evidence: minor senses

There are also some less frequent meanings, extensions, and specializations, which I would like to clear out of the way before returning to examine the main patterns in greater detail. They are all related semantically to the first meaning, 'surrender'.

The first of these is roughly glossed as 'collapse'. Most examples are rather technical, as the following show:

And then to see whether that does reach the yield stress for plastic deformation or not ... (7)

You see if it does. Then it will yield just the same way as a tensile specimen ... (2)

There are eleven clear instances of this sense, and two related ones. To avoid fragmentation of the general picture at this point, I shall return to further discussion of this category at the end of this chapter.

Another minor sense can be glossed as 'soft'. It is exemplified in two cases only, both of *yielding* used as a predicative adjective:

... the main thoroughfare. The crowd was not as yielding. The groups of young men called out in ... (80)

Feathers are heavier and cheaper. Foam is less yielding, more springy doesn't last as long as do ... (87)

Finally, a lone example of *yields* being used of the indistinct boundary between districts in a city:

... of Brompton Road and Thurloe Place Knightsbridge yields insensibly to South Kensington. The ... (116)

Here the meaning of 'surrender' has altogether vanished in a weakly metaphorical use.

There are not nearly enough examples of these minor meanings for us to attempt generalizations. A different selection of texts might have produced more instances of one, less of another. But they serve to exemplify something that has emerged from every single study of concordances—that the different meanings of a word have very different frequencies. Chapter 6 exploits this point.

Counter-examples: general

Let us return to the major patterning, and point to a frequent coincidence of sense and structure. In 33 of the 125 cases, the first meaning, 'give way' is realized by an intransitive verb. In 30 cases, the second meaning, 'produce', is realized by a noun. In at least 15 clear cases of the third meaning, 'leads to', the word is a transitive verb. This last figure could rise to over 20, following the discussion below.

Taking the most cautious figures, this alignment of sense and structure covers 75 of the 125 occurrences of the lemma *yield*, or 60 per cent. The minor meanings that have been discussed account for 16 examples, and there is one unclassified example (92), so the proportion is more realistically 75 out of 108, or practically 70 per cent.

It certainly seems worthwhile to examine the cases which are not aligned in this way, to see if there are any circumstances of note, or whether they are clear counter-examples. Text analysis takes a much more relaxed attitude to counter-examples than grammar does. There are many reasons why an odd or unusual structure can occur in a text; in a written text, it can be an accident of production or editing; in a spoken text, it can result from a momentary slip in control or a perception of suddenly changed circumstances; in both, it can be a quirk of the user, or a deliberately unusual expression. There can also be unusual phrases when people are describing unusual events, or when they become self-conscious about language.

Such oddities can safely be discarded when we are preparing generalizations. They come into their own in other studies, for example literary studies, where their unusual quality is invested with particular significance. But those literary studies rest on implicit or explicit reference to norms, and the present work is concerned with the establishment of such norms.

Thus, we search for recurrent patterning, for similarities, for mutual reinforcement. Examples which do not toe the line we scrutinize in the search for some explanation of their oddity.

Counter-examples: first sense

Of the 49 cases where *yield* means 'give way', 33 show *yield* as an intransitive verb, and 16 show it as a transitive verb. Let us examine these 16 cases.

In 6 of them, *yield* is followed by *up* and these are the only cases of *up* following immediately after *yield*. *Up* appears to be acting semantically as a completive, but syntactically it appears to be acting to make a transitive structure sound natural. In three cases, the object is *secrets*, suggesting a rather specific phrase, and in one case (74) it seems to be a biblical echo. The examples are numbered 48, 49, 50 (yield), and 73, 74, 75 (yielded).

We can remove these 6 instances from the reckoning by saying that they indicate the existence of a transitive phrasal verb *to yield up*. The transitivity is associated with the particle *up* and not the particular sense of *yield*.

A hint of this is given in the dictionary quoted, which has another definition, scarcely distinguishable from the first, 'to surrender or relinquish, esp. as a result of force, persuasion etc.' But whereas the earlier definition is said to apply to an intransitive verb, and is 'sometimes followed by *to*', this is said to be transitive and 'often followed by *up*'.

Yield with an object

There are four remaining instances where *yield* occurs with an object:

> ... to no one, but they were obliged in the process to yield some fifteen to twenty kilometres. With ... (31)

> Any society that hopes to be stable must surely yield its most passionate prejudices in the cause ... (22)

> ... Soviet Union, remains adamant that it will not yield even a limited measure of editorial control ... (16)

> ... victory of the Cuban rebels, unwilling to yield the concessions that would defuse the ... (33)

It will be evident as we come to discuss individual examples that, in some instances, the quotation does not provide sufficient textual environment to settle the issue. It is possible to return to the original text, but the process is laborious, and it is most unlikely that pursuing a single example in this way will turn out to be worthwhile. If the need for an extended environment is clear from an early stage, then it can, of course, be provided—but at the cost of great clumsiness when one is handling large amounts of data. I shall discuss these in order of their apparent complexity:

Number 31: I interpret this example as having as direct object *some fifteen to twenty kilometres*, rather than as being an intransitive with an adverbial of distance. That is, the sense of 'give way' is maintained rather than the sense of 'retreat'. This seems to me to be an unusual use and I am not surprised that it is unique.

Number 22: I interpret this in the sense of 'abandon'. This is not a sense recognized in the dictionary and therefore it is presumably not a pattern to be followed.

Number 16: The word *surrender,* which we use to gloss this sense, has itself two main patterns: one reflexive-intransitive ('I surrender'), and one transitive, ('he surrendered his sword'). *Yield* seems to favour the first of these patterns, but this is a fairly clear example of the second. It could be that the author is beguiled by the phrase *limited measure,* which is a characteristic phrase used with the second sense, as will be seen in what follows.

Number 33: It is not clear from this short text whether concessions means 'land concessions', or the more general sense used in negotiations. The former meaning would suggest that this is a counter-example, but I interpret the concessions mentioned here as general. Therefore, *yield* is being used in the sense of 'abandon' and, as in example 22, constitutes a pattern that has no merit as a model of usage.

Yielding with an object

The form *yielding* occurs in approximately this sense of 'abandon' three times with an object:

... men who in 1958 had called him back to Power, by yielding Algeria to the Algerian nationalists ... (77)

... is to drive through a car cleaner. The bliss of yielding self and car to be soaped, washed and ... (90)

... should at least in part be conceded, or else of yielding to extremism what earlier was refused to ... (95)

Number 77: Again this is the 'abandon' sense against which I take a prescriptive stand. Of course, if many more examples occur one must concede that the language is moving in favour of such usage. In this material it is a minor variant.

Number 90: This is an unusual expression in a fanciful context, and can be seen as a one-off.

Number 95: A superficial reading of this could misinterpret the sequence yielding to extremism as 'giving way to extremism'. But the last few words of the example suggest strongly that there is a direct object which is a *what*-clause, placed late in the sentence to avoid ambiguity. It seems an odd example in a convoluted sentence.

Yielded with an object

The form *yielded* occurs in roughly this sense of 'abandon' three times with an object:

> ... more difficult to proceed; for the cattle droves yielded place then to mere foot-tracks from ... (63)

> ... for its young. The more complex animals, having yielded rigid instinctual behaviour for learning ... (65)

> ... Roman Catholics lived in Rome, but Barber never yielded the point. He was particularly touchy ... (66)

Number 63: This seems to be a variant of the phrase 'gave place to' and has no parallel in the data.

Number 65: The syntax seems to be muddled and non-standard—to yield *x* for *y* almost in the sense of 'exchange': a unique usage in the corpus.

Number 66: This collocation of *yield* and *point* sounds fairly plausible, but it is the only example. Perhaps a much larger corpus would show this as a phrase of growing regularity.

These are all the potential counter-examples to the first sense, and I conclude that they do not constitute a case of any strength against the basic coincidence of sense and structure. No example fully survives scrutiny, and only number 16 is a starter for a counter-example. They range from what might be small mistakes or rough usage, through what is probably artistic deviation, and are subject to the distorting influence of strongly established phrases and sense associations.

Descriptive and prescriptive study

In recent years, descriptive and prescriptive studies of language have been thought of as arising from polarized, irreconcilable positions. Text study obliges us to relate them to each other, because a purely objective description of a text will not contain adequate generalization, and an exclusively prescriptive account will not engage the evidence satisfactorily.

In this account, the prescriptive stance is of necessity subjective, relying only on the crudest frequency statistics. Meanwhile, work advances towards the establishment of a more objective method of classifying occurrences (see Chapter 6). The evidence is initially statistical, but is subjected to the application of a linguistic principle such as the alignment of sense and structure. The result should be a powerful evaluative argument.

Texts contain many examples of typical language patterns, but there are also many extended, displaced, and distorted usages. We must find a way of isolating these. When we have only one or two occurrences to go on, we cannot distinguish formally between *ad hoc* usages and indications of forthcoming change.

Further study will lead to better statement of principle, but it is unlikely that subjective judgement can be dispensed with. Eventually, structural statement contains an element of what should be the case, which can contrast with what is the case. Prescriptive studies fall into disrepute only when they ignore or become detached from evidence.

In this chapter, the pursuit of individual examples to show their deviance is undertaken simply to establish norms. The only examples which come under criticism are those which deviate from the tentative norms for no discernible reason. Even then, they may constitute evidence of some historical change which is obscured from the view of the synchronic analyst. It may be that these examples show the beginnings of an extension of what things can be yielded.

The advantage of stressing the norms is considerable in many applications of linguistic description. It is, of course, standard practice in language teaching, though the norms which are currently taught need considerable revision. Stating the basic regularities does not preclude a user deviating from them—in fact, it aids the process. The notion of Productive Features (Sinclair *et al.* 1990) shows how corpus study can identify places where a user of English has an open-ended set of options.

Counter-examples: second and third senses

To return to the description of the lemma *yield*, the transitive verbs are again the problem area.

Yield as transitive verb

There are five pretty clear examples of *yield* used in the sense 'produce', as a transitive verb:

> ... marginal peasant's holding of 0.23 acres would yield only 200 pounds of rice or less. Annual ... (28)

It 'felt' harder because the exhausted soil was yielding less, so there was less plant cover for ... (86)

It had been cultivated the year before but had yielded very little. Moumoni said he didn't ... (76)

... than recoup these costs from the extra harvest yielded: but in the meantime he needs credit to ... (57)

... will spend every penny - and more - that is yielded by taxes. A cut in taxes will mean a cut ... (58)

The first example (28) has all the features of the nominal usage, and along with the others obliges us to recognize a secondary structure with a weakly transitive verb, which could be interpreted as an adverbial or as an object; the latter seems more plausible. The same goes for example 76. The other examples are two of the three occurrences of *yielded* in the passive. Passive voice confirms the transitivity potential of the verb.

Doubtful cases

There are eight doubtful examples. In two of them my judgement tends towards the 'produce' sense:

... against it. The traditional human IQ tests yield a score which runs between 0 and an upper ... (9)

... of water. Only two domestic baths-full would yield an incredible solid pound of bacteria. The ... (12)

In example 9, the point is that tests are expected to produce scores— that is what they are for; although the results are not physical, like grain, this example makes a strong claim to our second, more specific sense. So also example 12, though the oddity of the measurement in 'baths-full' and 'pounds of bacteria' make it a highly idiosyncratic usage.

In the other 6 doubtful cases, the balance, in my judgement, swings the other way; the nearest sense is the third one, more 'leads to' than 'produce deliberately':

... electrical significance, but which did not seem to yield any satisfactory bell ringing inside, or ... (13)

... painted in front, where the dry dust refused to yield even a weed. Above the picture, stamped in ... (15)

... agreed prices which they knew were very likely to yield profits that the Ministry would not regard ... (29)

... economics supplies only one - whether a thing yields a money profit to those who undertake it ... (101)

... an activity carried on by a group within society yields a profit to society as a whole. Even ... (102)

... are allowed to change. The rent control board yields them an extra seven and a half per cent ... (121)

Example 13 is one of those which would need more textual environment if we were to hunt down its exact sense; but there is enough in the citation to suggest that it is a quizzical usage and far from typical. Example 15 shares features with 28, 76, and particularly 86, but there is no sense of a deliberate attempt to cultivate crops.

The next three examples show a collocation of *yield* and *profit* which may well be best dealt with as a phrase in its own right. Although several other examples (55, 58, and 121) deal with money acquired through trade, it is not identified as profit or named as such.

There remains example 121, which is the only double transitive, and which is used in an unusual sense, something like 'allows them to charge or acquire'. Without a fuller citation, it is difficult to be precise about this example, but it is an atypical usage both syntactically and semantically.

We can conclude from this that, whereas this meaning is overwhelmingly realized as a noun (30 cases), it is possible to use it occasionally as a transitive verb.

First minor sense

At this point, I should like to return to the first 'minor' sense, where I quoted examples 7 and 2 earlier. Like example 7 are several others (the first two are the same stretch of text, within which *yield stress* occurs twice):

... You will get yielding then when the yield stress the average yield stress v divided ... (4)

... yielding then when the yield stress the average yield stress v divided by the area. Which is a ... (5)

... and that will collapse essentially when the yield stress the average stress across here is ... (6)

... is being stretched until you reach the yield stress and then it starts to yield ... (8)

In these cases, the form *yield* is chosen and the syntactic position is that of a noun modifier of another noun. *Yield* also occurs in this sense as a verb, as we saw in example 3, and also 2 (see below):

You see if it does. Then it will yield just the same way as a tensile specimen ... (2)

The form *yielding* occurs in this sense as a noun head:

... the Tresco and von Meses er criteria of yielding what are they? Well come on ... (82)

... the direct stress. Criteria of yielding based on the maximum value of the ... (78)

... the er stresses on the body t: Criteria of yielding in that he's asking under the action of ... (79)

... small couple here and you will get yielding then when the yield stress the average ... (81)

There is a less technical but very similar sense of *yielded* in example 72:

... self with outstretched arms as the flesh and bone yielded under his weight. Oh God, there was a ... (72)

Finally, in this sense, there is an extension of this meaning in example 47, which might also be seen as an extension of our first meaning—that is, 'surrender'. With a single example, the point is not worth pursuing:

... to a filing cabinet. The latter, however, will yield to a jemmy and a bit of brute force, while ... (47)

At first sight, this evidence runs counter to the prevailing argument which is advanced in this chapter. The sense has been dubbed 'minor' yet accounts for over 10 per cent of the examples and runs numerically close to the third of the so-called 'main' senses (see Table 1, in Appendix III at the back of the book). It occurs in three different structural roles with a small number of examples of each.

On closer examination, however, it can be seen to be a minor pattern which offers too little evidence for detailed analysis. It has been pointed out that the dominant usage is technical, and a special kind of phrase,

64

the technical term (Yang forthcoming), accounts for most of the examples. *Yield stress* occurs four times and *criteria of yielding* occurs three times. The dictionary gives *yield stress* as a separate headword. The remaining four instances are intransitive verb usages or (in example 81) a nominalization of that, and can be assimilated as mildly technical extensions of the first main sense.

The descriptive problem here illustrates a feature of language which must be taken to be inherent—no matter how thorough and comprehensive a study is, there is always a lot left over for an even more detailed study. Consequently, if we were to collect sufficient instances of this technical sense, there is no reason to believe that such fuller evidence would contradict the basic argument of this chapter.

Conclusion

All the occurrences of *yield* have now been covered, except one:

> ... old breeze across the oceanic warmths of the ever yielding sub-continent. Even his shabby clothes ... (92)

No doubt if we traced this back to source it could be illuminated; as one indeterminate example in 125 it can remain to remind us that all interpretation is partial.

The final picture can be tabulated as follows: Table 1 gives a summary and Table 2 (also in Appendix III, at the back of the book) gives references to the actual instances, which are given in the Appendix.

It seems that there is a strong tendency for sense and syntax to be associated.

The correspondences are overwhelming. Most of this chapter has been concerned with the various classes of exception, doubtful usage, etc., obscuring the regularity that is clearly displayed. This study supports the contention that adjustment of meaning and structure is a regular feature of a language. It can be used to provide valuable evidence for lexicography, suggesting sense divisions, and identifying phrase units with distinctive patterning. Then, by using the same evidence in reverse, the traditional domain of syntax will be invaded by lexical hordes.

5
Words and phrases

Introduction

The studies of *decline* and *yield* in the previous two chapters open up the possibility of associating grammar and vocabulary in ways that can improve the description of both. They are both rich in semantic associations.

In this chapter and the next, we explore the use of concordances in the description of words that are much more frequent than so-called 'vocabulary words'. They are not normally expected to have a strong lexical environment, but are more associated with the grammatical end of the spectrum. The objectives are to demonstrate:

- how carefully the language is patterned;
- how the description is very sensitive to the number of instances of a form;
- how criteria for meaning (see Chapter 4) are applied in a specific case.

In addition, the relevance of this research to the teaching and learning of English is pointed up by the consideration of a feature of English much dreaded by learners—phrasal verbs.

Phrasal verbs

The choice of an example to illustrate the argument of this chapter was, as usual, partly accidental, and partly deliberate. I was looking for a fairly common, rather dull little word that was comparatively neglected in description and in teaching. I found out by chance that the word *set* was not well regarded by some experienced teacher–colleagues, and noticed that it got scant treatment in the syllabuses that I was able to examine. The immediate presumption was that it was a difficult word to isolate semantically. 'What does *set* mean?' is hardly a sensible question. It has to be put into context, because in most of its usage it contributes to meaning in combination with other words.

Among the many combinations of *set* are a number of phrasal verbs, such as *set about, set in, set off*, and these are picked out in language teaching as offering exquisite problems to the learner. The reason for their causing problems is easily explained. The co-occurrence of two quite common little words can unexpectedly create a fairly subtle new meaning that does not seem to be systematically related to either or both of the original words. The disposition of the words involved, and their syntax, is governed by complex and unpredictable rules.

The prospect sounds formidable even for native speakers, yet they not only manage phrasal verbs with aplomb, but seem to prefer them to single word alternatives. In fact, the whole drift of the historical development of English has been towards the replacement of words by phrases, with word-order acquiring greater significance.

Some recent work (Sinclair, Moon *et al.* 1989) shows that the semantics of phrasal verbs is not as arbitrary as it is often held to be. We usually cite phrasal verbs based on the verb element (*give up, give out, give over*, etc.). If, instead, we group them by the particle (*give over, get over, tide over*), it is possible to make sense groupings.

It will, however, be a long time before people will routinely look up *give over* in a dictionary under *over* rather than *give*. The presentation in this chapter emphasizes the importance of the environment of *set* in determining the meaning. In the first instance, a particle following raises the prospect of a phrasal verb; then, the other words around help in indicating the precise meaning.

Some numerical facts

In the corpus of approximately 7.3 million words, used in Chapters 3 and 4, there are 2,320 instances of the different forms of the lemma *set*. We associate together the forms *set, sets*, and *setting* as instances of the word *set*, and the frequency of each is:

set	1885	(80%)
sets	219	(9%)
setting	246	(11%)

Other possible associates such as *setter* and *settee* are ignored.

Set is thus one of the commonest words in the language—the uninflected form is ranked number 272. However, if we compare the relative frequency of the inflected forms *sets* and *setting*, we see that they are not nearly as common as *set*, being approximately 9 per cent and 11 per cent of the lemma.

This is a commonly observed pattern, where one of the forms is much more common than any other. Similar, if less dramatic, tendencies are shown for *decline* and *yield* in Chapters 3 and 4 respectively. This means that if *sets* or *setting* has a use which is not shared by *set*, we have much less evidence to go on. Whatever criteria we use, there is nearly ten times as much evidence available for *set*.

It could be argued that, in one respect at least, the inflection of *set* is untypical, and that the frequency of forms of *set* will reflect the oddity. *Set* is one of a handful of verbs in English which do not have a separate past tense form. So whatever frequency is assigned to *walk* and *walked*, *say* and *said*, etc. is not differentiated in *set*. To complicate the picture further, all three forms of the lemma *set* are also readily available as nouns, and the picture is not at all straightforward.

However, compared to the vast majority of words, even the least common form *sets* is generously represented. But when we look for combinations of even these frequent words, the expectations are not promising.

If a corpus is held to be representative of the language as a whole, the probability of occurrence of a word-form can be expressed in general as a relation between the frequency of the word-form in the corpus and the total number of word-forms in the corpus.

In the case of *set* this is:

$$\frac{1855}{7,300,000} \quad \text{or } 0.00025$$

This means that the chance of *set* being the next word in the text is about 250 per million, or one occurrence in every 3,935 words.

Combinations of *set* + particle

How common are the phrasal verbs with *set*? *Set* is particularly rich in making combinations with words like *about, in, up, out, on, off*, and these words are themselves very common.

As an example, how likely is *set off* to occur, whether phrasal verb or not? Both are frequent words; *off* occurs approximately 556 times in a million words. Its probability of being the next word is 0.00055. We must now multiply the probabilities of *set* and *off*, because the question we are asking can be roughly rephrased as follows: how likely is *off* to occur immediately after *set*? This is approximately 0.00025 x 0.00055, which gives us the minute figure of 0.0000001375.

Two important considerations are left out of this calculation, one linguistic and the other statistical.

a. the phrasal verb *set off* can have a noun group inside it, for example: It was the hedge which *set* the garden *off*.

There are very few of these and so they have little effect on the general numerical argument.

b. The assumption behind this calculation is that the words are distributed at random in a text. It is obvious to a linguist that this is not so, and a rough measure of how much *set* and *off* attract each other is to compare the probability with what actually happens.

In a text of 7.3 million words distributed at random, we might expect 0.0000001375 x 7,300,000 occurrences of *set off*, that is, one only. Since there are several different phrasal verbs with the form *set off*, and no doubt some occurrences of *set* followed by *off* which do not provide an instance of a phrasal verb, we might require a fairly large number of occurrences of the combination of forms to show the characteristic patterns. At a frequency of about 1 in 7 million, we would require to collect large amounts of text, running into the hundreds of millions of words.

The gloomy picture thus projected by our arithmetic is, in fact, considerably relieved by what we find in actual texts. This is because our initial assumption, that the words are distributed at random, is false. *Set off* occurs nearly seventy times in the 7.3 million-word corpus, as against the random prediction of only one occurrence. The 70 instances give us enough evidence of the main patterning.

The combination *set in*

In this central part of the chapter, I shall consider all the instances of *set, sets,* and *setting* followed by *in*. The different ways in which the occurrence of these words together contribute to meanings will emerge, and the evidence will be found to be mainly in the surrounding language.

We begin by gathering all instances of the sequence *set in*. There are 90 of them. To this we add: *sets in* (16); *setting in* (6); and, for the sake of completeness, *settings in* (2). The total of instances of a form of *set* followed immediately by *in* is thus 114.

The first analysis combines several steps:

- noting the word class of each example;
- classifying the meaning roughly into word-meaning and phrase-meaning;
- assigning the word-meanings to senses, where possible;
- working out the phrases;
- assigning the phrase-meanings to senses.

The distinction of word-meaning and phrase-meaning is of considerable importance in language study, and is explained in some detail in Chapter 8. Intuitively, we feel that some instances of a word are quite independently chosen, while in other cases we feel that the word combines with others to deliver a single multi-word unit of meaning. We shall call word-meaning *independent*, and phrase-meaning *dependent*.

In between these two fixed points is collocation, where we see a tendency for words to occur together though they remain largely independent choices. In what follows, the 114 instances are divided into:

- Nouns
- Verbs
  - sense (i)
  - sense (ii)
  - minor sense
  - sundry idioms
- Phrasal verbs

Let us first dispose of a few instances that do not fit into the above classification. There are five of these, one a typographical error (*as-sets*) and one where even the twenty-word citation does not give enough evidence of its meaning. Two are instances of other idioms with *set*, but in the passive so that *set* is immediately followed by *in*, for example:

He was asking *a precedent* to be *set* in a field where ...

The last is:

... the controlled fires he *sets* in spring devastate shrubs ...

We now go on to examine the first five categories in the above classification, before giving fuller attention to *set in* as a phrasal verb.

71

Nouns

The use of *set* as a noun includes all four forms of the lemma:

set	6 out of 90 (7%)
sets	4 out of 16 (25%)
setting	5 out of 6 (83%)
settings	2 out of 2 (100%)

Both instances of *settings* are nominal, of course. All but one of *setting* are nominal, which suggests that the verb is not much used in the progressive tense. Collocations include *work setting, social setting, a suitable setting. Sets* as a noun includes *television sets*, and *chemistry sets. Set* as a noun includes: *the social set, the Martini set, theatre set, a fishing set,* and *a TV set.*

These are all characteristic nominal uses of *set* which have been captured because they happen to be immediately followed by *in*. They would be best treated in a description of the whole nominal pattern of *set*. Here we merely note them and clear them out of the way.

Verbs

Among the verbal uses, there are two principal independent senses and two minor ones. Only the form *set* occurs—not even *sets*, suggesting a preponderance of past-tense usage.

Sense (i)
There are 25 instances of *set* followed by *in* and meaning approximately 'placed'. Seven are to do with physical position (including one about someone who *had his bones set in an awmbry*; only the OED was able to tell me that an awmbry was a kind of cupboard, and this was not an instance of bonesetting). Twelve more are to do with the disposition of buildings, streets, etc. Three are abstract placings (for example, 'high expectations, set in the commercial future for nuclear power'); two are variations of a well-known quotation (including the remarkable 'no man, or woman, is an island, set in a silver sea'). One is a figurative extension, 'set in a haze of blue'.

Sense (ii)
There are 18 instances of *set* followed by *in*, meaning approximately 'located', and characteristically used of plays, films, and stories, such as:

Clearly, the film, set in Glasgow and the Highlands ...

Minor senses
Of the two minor independent senses of *set*, one is to do with type-setting and the other is *set in my memory*, which means in context 'fixed in place' and not just 'placed'.

In all the above verbal instances, the words *set* and *in* make an important collocation, and not the casual co-occurrence that was found in the nominal uses.

Sundry idioms
There are 20 instances of uses which I have termed idiomatic, because in addition to *set* and *in* there are other restrictions as well.

a. Of these, six have *set in* followed by a possessive pronoun and the word *ways*, such as:
   ... too old and *set in her ways* ever to change.
b. Five are of the phrase *set in motion*.
c. The remainder are one or two instances of *set in train, set in hand, set in order, set in a traditional mould, set in front of, set in juxtaposition to,* and *set in the balance*.

This group of idioms comprises items for which a much larger text corpus would be needed to see if it was justifiable to pick them out as I have done here. They all seem common enough, and it is a slight shock to see how rare they are in a large corpus—one has to keep in mind the extreme unlikelihood, on statistical grounds, of any of them occurring at all.

Set in as a phrasal verb

Up to this point, we have been merely clearing the ground for study of the phrasal verb *set in*. The original 114 instances of *set* followed by *in* are reduced to 29. Three of the four forms are involved, as follows:

set	16 out of 90 (18%)
sets	10 out of 16 (63%)
setting	1 out of 6 (17%)

The phrasal verb meaning is that if something *sets in*, it begins, and seems likely to continue and develop.

One of the first things to note about the phrasal verb is that it seems to occur typically in a small and/or minor part of a sentence. It is not easy to say exactly what gives this feeling but the following may be factors.

1 The clauses in which *set in* is chosen are in general rather short—six words or fewer in the main. The longer ones are longer because of an adjunct rather than the subject, which is in most cases a single word or an article and noun pair.

2 A number of the clauses are subordinate. With the samples available, it is not possible to assign status in every case, and there are some of clear main clauses; but I think the tendency to lower status should be noted.

3 *Set in* is final in the clause in 22 of the 29 cases, and sentence-final in nine of them, showing a clear tendency to end structures.

Observations such as those above are difficult to evaluate because we lack comparative stylistic data, but the following is a very typical example:

... where the rot *set in* ...

Word-forms

As suggested in 1 above, the majority of verbal groups are simple, containing just the form of *set*. All the occurrences of *sets* (10) are, of course, in the present tense, and at least nine of these deal with general states of affairs rather than the here-and-now. None of them is unambiguously in a main clause, where the tense choice relates directly to time.

Of the others, the vast majority are in the narrative past—either simple past (9) or pluperfect with *had* (4). There are single instances of *would, has,* and *was,* and one complex verb *started to set in* which again shows the narrative past.

From this we can conclude that there is a tendency towards reference to things past or things which are not sensitive to the passage of time, which goes reasonably well with the meaning of the phrase; the phrasal verb is not used in speculation about the future, or in statements about the present. For example:

It was no wonder that disillusion *had set in* ...

Subjects

The most striking feature of this phrasal verb is the nature of the subjects. In general, they refer to unpleasant states of affairs. Only three refer to the weather; a few are neutral, such as *reaction* and *trend*. The main vocabulary is *rot, decay, malaise, despair, ill-will, decadence, impoverishment, infection, prejudice, vicious (circle), rigor mortis, numbness, bitterness, mannerism, anticlimax, anarchy, disillusion, disillusionment, slump.* Not one of these is conventionally desirable or attractive.

The subjects of *set in* are also, as can be seen above, largely abstractions: several are nominalizations of another part of speech.

A dictionary entry

These observations characterize the phrase and illustrate its use. In a dictionary, a great deal of information has to be compressed into a couple of lines and it must be reasonably easy to read. The explanation given in the *Collins COBUILD English Language Dictionary* is:

> If something unpleasant *sets in*, it begins and seems likely to continue or develop.

The three examples cited in the dictionary illustrate many of the points made in this section. *A feeling of anticlimax set in*; the subject is one of the longer ones, but is abstract and fairly unpleasant. *It must be treated quickly before infection sets in* illustrates the very short subordinate clause with the present tense verb. *The bad weather has set in for the winter* is one of a small but distinctive group of concrete subjects that would very likely be recognized as appropriate by native speakers.

Not all the analytical points can be covered in such a short summary. Dictionary compilers have to work at a greater pace than the analyst, and they have to pay attention to a broad range of features. *Set in* is one of 79 paragraphs in the Cobuild dictionary about *set*. However, it is worth noting that the short entry picks out typical features and offers sound examples. This analysis was done from the concordances as a separate exercise from the dictionary compilation, so it gives some idea of the amount of information assimilated and evaluated during the compilation of a dictionary.

Other phrasal verbs with *set*

In a less detailed examination of phrasal verbs with *set*, a similar range and type of specialization can be observed.

The phrasal verb *set about* is interesting in that it is regularly followed by an *-ing* form of another verb. The second verb is normally transitive, so the framework 'set about doing something' is appropriate. In front of the phrasal verb, there are a number of structures concerning uncertainty: negatives and *how*; questions with *how* or *who*; modal *would*; phrases like *little idea, the faintest idea, I'm not sure, evidently not knowing*. For example:

She had not the faintest idea of how to set about earning any.

The context in many cases is that of problem solving, which explains the oddity of saying that someone 'set about making a cup of coffee'. Less obvious is the tendency for this construction to be used to refer to a subsidiary aim within a grander design. 'We set about X in order, ultimately to achieve Y'. The length of a citation makes it impossible to demonstrate this tendency very clearly, but here is a characteristic example:

The enemy had to set about securing his flanks and rear before ...

Set apart and *set aside* are similar in meaning, but not in usage. *Set apart* is characteristically passive, with the agent phrase, but with a prepositional phrase introduced by *from*. The emphasis is on the state of apartness and the status and quality of whatever has been selected for apartness. One example sums it up with *set apart and above from the rest*.

Set aside is more concerned with the activity of separating, or the separation itself. So, in the majority of instances, it is actually stated who sets the thing aside. Instead of acquiring distinction by being *set aside*, the phrase can be used for rejection: 'So rare a thing that it is not to be lightly set aside'. There are hardly any instances where *set apart* and *set aside* can be interchanged, even though their meaning is so similar.

The combination *set off* has several uses in informal English. The main one—twice as common as the next—is to do with starting a journey. The verb is intransitive and is followed in nearly every case by a prepositional phrase which tells us about the journey, its direction, or destination; very often the preposition is *on, for, in, into*. A secondary structure is a *to*-infinitive, following a phrasal verb telling us about the journey. These continuations are, of course, optional, but it is noticeable that in nearly every case there is one. For example:

We set off in his car on the five-thousand-mile journey.

76

In the other prominent use of *set off* the verb is transitive. The meaning is to do with starting anything from an explosion to a train of thought. Very few of the examples refer to physical explosions: there are several where the object is much more abstract: 'a new *round of* –', 'a whole *series of* – ', 'a monstrous *escalation of* – ', 'a reaction'. A typical example of this use is:

In Austria the broadcast was to set off a *train of* thought and actions.

One prominent feature of this use is that the object of the phrasal verb nearly always refers to something new. This is most clearly seen in the choice of article in front of the noun, which is characteristically the indefinite article *a*. Even the two instances of *the* are both of the type which express a generalization:

The spark which set off *the* explosion ...

... and so set off *the* charge for the black revolution.

In neither case does the italicized *the* refer back to a previously indentified item.

The phrasal verb *set out* can also be used to refer to the start of a journey, in the same way as *set off* can, but this is not its most frequent use. In nearly half of all occurrences, it signifies intention, and is followed by a *to*-infinitive starting a clause. For example:

Babbage *set out to build* a full scale working version.

The *to*-infinitive is transitive. The remaining examples are fairly evenly divided between reference to the start of a journey (regularly followed by *on* or *for*) and a meaning close to 'expound':

The report set out the alternatives.

This is a transitive phrasal verb; half of its occurrences are in the passive. The things which are set out include: *agenda, items, criteria, themes, hopes, lists, stages, theory, argument, programme.*

The last phrasal verb I want to mention is *set up*, and I only want to draw attention here to the same feature of newness which was noted in the discussion of *set off*. In the many cases where *set up* is followed by an object, the vast majority show a noun group which has an indefinite determiner, or, being plural, no determiner at all.

Conclusion

The notes above on other phrasal verbs with *set* underline the points made in detail for *set in*. Each sense of the phrase is co-ordinated with a pattern of choice that helps to distinguish it from other senses. Each is particular; it has its uses and its characteristic environment. There is no need to present the information as a featureless list of phrasal verbs with no guidance as to which is which and why they are preferable to single words.

The distinguishing criteria are commonplace features of grammar or semantics, and even in the small group of phrasal verbs with *set*, we can see them beginning to recur. The prospect arises of being able to present the facts of the language in a much more precise way than before. Instead of individual words and phrases being crudely associated with a 'meaning', we could see them presented in active and typical contexts, and gradually freed from those contexts to enjoy, in most cases, a severely limited autonomy. Very few common words are thought to have a residue of patterning that can be used independently.

Since phrasal verbs are said to be extremely difficult to learn, we may review what significance this descriptive exercise has for the learner. The material in this chapter is not intended for direct exploitation in the classroom (though all students respond well to being offered corpus data). It is gradually building up, as a database for teachers' reference, a repository of facts about English on which new syllabuses and materials can be based.

If *set in train* always occurs together in this sequence when it has the obvious meaning, then the three words constitute one choice. As soon as learners have appreciated that each phrase operates as a whole, more or less as a single word, then the difficulty disappears and they have a new word *set in train*. Not many learners will confuse *set* and *say* just because they begin with *s*; learners are not expecting *s* to have meaning on its own. Once it is clear that what matters is the meaning of the phrase as a whole, then any recollection of the independent meanings of the constituent words will reinforce the phrase meaning.

Many of the above observations are probabilistic—they show strong tendencies in the behaviour of words rather than clear-cut alternatives. However, it would be misleading to think that these are radically different from the familiar grammatical patterns. Grammar is not easily applied to text, despite the claims that are sometimes made.

Exceptions, gradations, continua, and the like are commonplace. Likewise, the descriptions that start with text will gradually find reasons for apparent exceptions, and expose generalities.

The evidence that is accumulating suggests that learners would do well to learn the common words of the language very thoroughly, because they carry the main patterns of the language. The patterns have to be rather precisely described in order to avoid confusions, but then are capable of being rather precisely deployed.

At present, many learners avoid the common words as much as possible, and especially where they make up the idiomatic phrases. Instead of using them, they rely on larger, rarer, and clumsier words which make their language sound stilted and awkward. This is certainly not their fault, nor is it the fault of the teachers, who can only work within the kind of language descriptions that are available.

Now we can have access to much more reliable information, and learners will be able to produce with confidence much more idiomatic English, with less effort involved.

6

The meeting of lexis and grammar

Introduction

This chapter considers what is involved in making a description of the very common words of a language, using the new techniques described in this book. There are two main sets of factors:

a. those concerning how information about the word is gathered, evaluated, and organized;
b. those concerning the presentation of the information in a reference work.

What is said about *of*

First of all, let us review common practice. It is often said that very common words just waste space in a dictionary, that their proper place is in a grammar, and that no one would ever look them up in a dictionary.

The entries in most dictionaries are indeed not very helpful about words like, *the, of, and*—the most common words in the language. Because dictionaries traditionally give priority to semantic meaning, as against the meaning found in grammar, usage, and pragmatics, they try to analyse the words by semantic criteria. This is a difficult task, indeed, these very words are frequently said to lack semantic meaning altogether. One dictionary gathers the following examples of *of* in one category of meaning:

the city of York
the art of painting
the age of eight
the problem of unemployment
a price increase of 15 per cent
some fool of a boy

Using the hallowed criterion of substitutability (that is, that the definition can actually replace *of* in the text), it defines *of* in this sense as *that is/are; being.* It is difficult to imagine in what circumstances a person will need this information. Another dictionary collects examples like:

cure sb. of a disease
rid a warehouse of rats
rob sb. of his money
relieve sb. of his anxiety

These are dubbed as 'indicating relief, deprivation, riddance'. It seems more likely that such an indication is given in the verb (*cure, rid,* etc.), rather than in the *of.*

It might, then, be thought that a more helpful account of a word like *of* would be found in grammar books. Since its main contribution to the language appears to be its participation in grammatical structure, there should be a tidy treatment of it in any reasonable grammar.

Sad to say, this is not the case. *Of* pops up all over the place, attracting dozens of special statements. It does not readily fit a conventional grammar any more than it fits a conventional dictionary. In one recent grammar there are over fifty references to *of,* spanning the entire book with substantial entries in more than half the chapters.

In this grammar, there seems to be an implied distinction between an '*of*-phrase', as in partitives like 'a gallon of water', and prepositional phrases, which are dealt with elsewhere in the book (Quirk *et al.* 1985, Chapters 5 and 9).

In a well-known pedagogical grammar, there are fourteen references to *of,* fairly evenly spread over the first hundred pages. Twelve of these references concern the patterns preceding *of,* and only two ('possessives' and *of all*) concern what follows *of* (Thomson and Martinet 1986).

Despite this scattered distribution, everyone seems unanimous that it is a preposition. However, it does not seem to be at all a typical preposition. In one grammar, for instance, it appears at the beginning of the chapter on prepositions and then drops out until some fairly minor uses are swept up towards the end (Quirk *et al.* 1985, Chapter 9).

A corpus view of *of*

Prepositions are principally involved in combining with following nouns to produce prepositional phrases which function as adjuncts in clauses. This is not anything like the main role of *of*, which combines with preceding nouns to produce elaborations of the nominal group. So whereas typical instances of the preposition *in* and *behind* are:

... in Ipswich ...
... in the same week ...
... behind the masks ...

Typical instances of *of* are:

... the back of the van ...
... a small bottle of brandy ...

It is true that *of* occasionally heads a prepositional phrase which functions as an adjunct, for example,

I think of the chaps on my film course ...
... convict these people of negligence.

However, the selection of *of* is governed by the choice of verb, and *of* is again sensitive to what precedes more than to what follows. And these instances constitute only a small proportion of the occurrence.

The value of frequency information shows itself here, because without it a grammar could conveniently introduce *of* as a plausible, ordinary preposition, and then add what in fact is its characteristic use as an extra. But with the overwhelming pattern of usage being in nominal groups, this fact must dominate any good description.

It may ultimately be considered distracting to regard *of* as a preposition at all. I can think of no parallel classification in language or anywhere else. We are asked to believe that the word which is by far the commonest member of its class (more than double the next) is not normally used in the structure which is by far the commonest structure for the class. Doubts about whether *be* should be considered a verb or not are not as serious as this.

It is not unreasonable to expect that quite a few of the very common words in a language are so unlike the others that they should be considered as unique, one-member word classes. If that status is granted to *of*, then there is no substantial difference between a dictionary entry for the word and a section of a grammar devoted to it. The one-member class is the place where grammar and lexis join.

The huge frequency of *of* means that there is no lack of evidence; in fact, in the present state of our ability to process language text, there is far too much evidence. Some kind of selection is necessary when *of* is approximately every fiftieth word—over two per cent of all the words—regardless of the kind of text involved.

The description offered below is the result of applying a simple procedure to deal with the embarrassment of examples. A selection of about thirty examples was retrieved arbitrarily from a large corpus, and on this evidence a tentative description was prepared. Then a second, similar set was retrieved and the description adjusted accordingly. After several such trawls, each new one added little to the picture, and it was felt that most of the major patterns had been exemplified, and quite a few minor ones as well.

To go beyond this requires either the application of a lot of labour or the creation of automatic routines. Before such investment, however, it is prudent to put the description forward for comment and criticism.

Frequency

This study is at a pilot stage and the actual frequency of instances of each category of use is not a reliable guide to the proportions in the language as a whole. The small samples showed hardly any consistency in the relative frequencies, and as usual most uses were exemplified in minute percentages.

However, even when the study advances to consider much more evidence, there will always be problems about statements of proportion and frequency. This is because a large number of examples are in one way or another problematic. One of the inescapable conclusions of studying real text is that the categories of description are so intertwined in realization that very few actual instances are straightforward illustrations of just one of the factors that led to the particular choice.

This does not constitute an argument for inventing examples; in fact, if carefully examined, it can be seen that this would develop into a total demolition of the view that people can replicate the real patterns of language outside their acts of communication. The selection of suitable examples for any particular explanation requires only a sufficiently large number of instances to choose from.

If many—sometimes most—of the actual instances show features that make them rather special, we are reminded of the fragility of any description, and the ever-present possibility that another way of organizing the evidence may lead to a superior description.

Of outside nominal groups

Around twenty per cent of the occurrence of *of* is not part of the regular structure of nominal groups. The main categories are:

a. a constituent of various set phrases, for example,
   of course; in spite of; out of; on top of; because of; consisting of; as a matter of fact; regardless of; in need of;

b. following certain verb-forms, for example,
   remind; constructed; sapped; made up; thought; smell; heard;

c. following certain adjectives, for example,
   short; capable; full.

Of in nominal groups

The simple structure of nominal groups is based on a headword which is a noun. Determiners, numerals, adjectives, etc. come in front of the noun and modify its meaning in various ways. Prepositional phrases and relative clauses come after the noun and add further strands of meaning.

The function of *of* is to introduce a second noun as a potential headword:

$$
\begin{array}{rcl}
\text{this kind} & \text{of} & \text{problem} \\
\text{the axis} & \text{of} & \text{rotation} \\
\text{the bottle} & \text{of} & \text{port} \\
\text{the treadmill} & \text{of} & \text{housework} \\
\text{leaves} & \text{of} & \text{trees}
\end{array}
$$

Each of the two nouns can support pre-modifiers, and the structural effect of these will be dealt with later in this chapter.

To begin with, we note that in most cases the second noun (N2) appears to be the most salient. This is not what would normally be expected in a conventional grammar; the general structure *the N1 of N2* would be analysed as having *N1* as headword, with *of N2* as a post-modifying prepositional phrase.

Conventional measures

Some grammars recognize that this kind of analysis is unhelpful when N1 is a number or a conventional measure:

both of them
a couple of weeks
one of my oldest friends
one of these occasions
millions of cats
three quarters of the world
another of these devices
a lot of the houses
some of those characteristics
a number of logistic support ships

Perhaps *any of 'em* could be added to this set. In all cases, N2 is the obvious headword.

Less conventional measures

We shall also attach to this set some more lexically rich partitives and quantifiers, which do not require special justification but indicate that this category, like most, has uncertain boundaries:

a series of S-shaped curves
the bulk of their lives
a fraction of a second
an average of 12.9 trout
groups of five
1,300 grams of cholesterol
the amount of sulphur dioxide
the bottle of port

In the last example, the classification here depends on interpreting *bottle* as more a measure rather than a physical object.

The status of headword

Before proceeding to more controversial cases, let us consider the status of headword, since the identification of headword is the first step in describing a nominal group.

The headword is the only obligatory element in the group, so it should not be capable of ready omission. Here we are not concerned with the niceties of syntax, or even concord, but with whether or not a listener or reader would be likely to follow the sense with one of the nouns missed out. Consider some examples (only the first is authentic):

86

a. Once I escaped the grasp of the undertow and had reached a rock ...
b. Once I escaped the grasp and had reached a rock ...
c. Once I escaped the undertow and had reached a rock ...

a. There are many examples of local authorities who've taken ...
b. There are many examples who've taken ...
c. There are many local authorities who've taken ...

a. By the evening of 5th August further enemy attacks had ...
b. By the evening further enemy attacks had ...
c. By the 5th August further enemy attacks had ...

In each of these cases, it is the omission of N2 that does the greatest damage to coherence, and **c.** is preferable to **b.**

A similar result is given by another criterion. It is reasonable to expect the headword of a nominal group to be the principal reference point to the physical world. In a large number of cases, N2 is the closer to a concrete physical object than N1:

the shapes of simple organisms
a glimpse of the old couple
the position of France

Focus nouns

Using these criteria, and expecting that it is normal for N2 to be the headword, the notion of quantifier or partitive can be extended into a general area of 'focus'.

Focus on a part

The first step is to include examples where N1 specifies some part of N2:

the middle of a sheet
the end of the nipple
the edge of the teeth
the top of the pillar
the end of the day
a part of us
that part of its power
the undersides of plates

Focus on a specialized part

This category of 'part' can be extended in various ways; for example, by more specialized words still indicating essentially a part of N2:

the evening of 5th August
the first week of the war
some green ends of onion
a small dried drop of it
the interior of Asia
the depths of the oceans
the point of detonation
in the midst of the grey gloom
the beginning of the world where winter is real
the outskirts of Hannover
leaves of trees
the horns of the bull

Focus on a component, aspect, or attribute

We move from 'part' to a more general notion of 'focus'. N1 specifies some component, aspect, or attribute of N2 which is relevant to the meaning of N2 in the context. Quite often, these are familiar idiomatic phrases:

the whole hull of your boat
the cream of the Cambridge theatre
an arrangement of familiar figures
the perils and labours of incubation
a uniform grouping of all arms
a little shrill gasp of shock
the recommendations of the Nunn–Bartlett Report
the text of two or three White House tapes
the disadvantages of wear and tear
generations of men
five thousand years of superstition, humbug and mumbo-jumbo
a list of the items
a little glimmer of satisfaction
the net of amateur or 'ham' radio stations
the sound of his feet
the new generation of cards
a fact of modern life

a sequence of zeroes and ones
the blistering heat of the prairie
their principles of operation
the headquarters of Sinn Fein
argument of the 'zero-growth' school
the study of geography

Some examples of this category have been reserved for special attention:

a. the portals of the Police Judiciary

This example shows N1 as almost redundant and present for stylistic reasons.

b. the forces of the Atlantic Alliance

In this example N1 also seems on the verge of being redundant, containing a kind of explicitness that is likely to have a tactical motive.

c. the granite of the Colorado Rockies

Assuming that the Colorado Rockies are made of granite, and that this is not a 'part' example, it is again virtually redundant and is motivated by stylistic considerations.

Support

The next major category is distinct from the 'focus' meaning because N1 is seen as offering some kind of support to N2, rather than just specifying some relevant aspect of N2. There are several ways in which this is done.

In some instances, N1 is a noun which is typically used as a supporting noun. Often reduced in meaning, words of this kind are noted in the *Collins COBUILD English Grammar* (Sinclair, Fox *et al.* 1990) as 'nouns which are rarely used alone':

the notion of machine intelligence
the position of France
an object of embarrassment
various kinds of economic sanctions
many examples of local authorities
the context of a kitchen
the familiar type of the peppery conservative

One colloquial development of this structure is a cover for vagueness, as exemplified by:

a sort of parody
the kind of thing that Balzac would have called
a sort of 'A' like that
some sort of madness
this kind of problem

Marginal to this category and the preceding one is the type where the support noun has considerable lexical force, but is subordinated by the structure, for example, 'the burden of partial occupation'.

In an interesting extension of this category, the support noun, N1, offers additional grammatical support.

In such an example as 'a single act of cheating', the support noun *act* offers its countability and 'noun-ness' to the participial *cheating*. The word *a* indicates the countability, and *single* the discreteness of the act. So, in this instance, *cheating* as one separate event is clearly distinguished from *cheating* as a settled habit or general disposition.

In another example, 'the power of speech', the support noun *power* is a familiar collocation and semantically almost redundant. It may help to focus on speech as a basic human faculty, but it is more important grammatically.

Metaphor

By the device of metaphor, another kind of support is offered to N2:

the juices of their imagination
the grasp of the undertow
a twilight of reason and language
the treadmill of housework

In each case, some semantic feature of N2 is pointed up by the metaphor of N1.

Double-headed nominal groups

In most of the above cases, N2 will be accepted as the headword (though see the discussion below, on modification of N1). But there remain many cases where neither noun seems to be pivotal or dominant, and where the structure simply requires both of them.

Titles

One minor type includes titles of people, places, etc. The first noun names someone or something that is affiliated to the institution named in N2:

the Duchess of Bedford
the United States of Europe
the new President of Zaire
the Garden of Allah

Nominalizations

Much more important, however, is the type where there is something approximating to a propositional relationship between the two nouns. The two nouns are understood as being in a 'verb–subject' or 'verb–object' kind of relationship.

The meaning of the structures can be brought out by composing clauses of equivalent meaning, for example, 'the payment of Social Security'. This is similar to a clause such as 'x pays Social Security' and N2 is in an 'object' relationship to N1.

Consider the following example, 'the enthusiastic collaboration of auctioneers'. In this example, related to 'Auctioneers collaborate enthusiastically', N2 is in a 'subject' relationship to N1.

Many grammars would explain these structures as clauses which had been somehow transformed into nominal groups, and indeed in a large number of cases N1 is a noun derived from a verb (*payment* from *pay*; *collaboration* from *collaborate*). It is, however, unnecessary to describe one structure as derived from another, and it is a complication which tends to ignore the function of *of*.

In general, we can say the following: the nominal group allows for two nouns to be chosen, of equal status and connected by *of*. These are interpreted as propositional, and the listener or reader deduces the likeliest propositional relationship. One consequence of using this construction is that N1 can be modified as a noun, whereas in the equivalent clause it would be modified as a verb.

Here is a representative collection of examples, including some which may be regarded as marginal or overlapping with another category:

the British view of the late senator
widespread avoidance of call-up
a wonderful sketch of her
the aim of the lateral thinker

                reflection of light
               the owner of the Estancia
          the description of the lady
             the growth of a single-celled creature
                   sales of its magazine
              advertising of infant formula
              the killing of civilians
     the spreading disillusion of Mrs Nixon's oldest supporters
            an exhibition of his work
      a superlative examiner of undergraduates
          the expectation of a million dollars
             the teaching of infants
                 control of the company
              the design of nuclear weapons
         a direct reflection of the openness
       the large movements of currency
        a clear reflection of the position

The main overlap is with the 'focus' category for N1, and we can recall
some of those examples which would not necessarily be out of place here:

          an arrangement of familiar figures
         a uniform grouping of all arms
         the recommendations of the Nunn–Bartlett Report
               the sound of his feet

Certainly, it is easy to find equivalent clauses for these examples ('X
arranges familiar figures', etc.). However, such an operation seems to
offer a misleading interpretation of the nominal group, as compared
with the 'focus' classification which relies on collocation (*recom-
mendation—report*) and the conventional associations we make in the
light of our experience of the world.

Another 'propositional' category arises when N1 is clearly derived
from an adjective, and this is understood as being in a complement
relation to N2 where N2 would be subject, for example, 'the shrewd-
ness of the inventor'. This is clearly relatable to a proposition such as
'the inventor was shrewd'.

The final type of 'double-headed' nominal group is the one that gives rise
to statements in grammars that associate *of* with possession. Because of
equivalences like, 'The cabinet of Dr Caligari', and 'Dr Caligari's Cabinet',
it is sometimes said that the N1 *of* N2 structure is an alternative way of

stating that N2 'possesses' N1. In fact, the *of* structure has little to do with ownership or possession, as can be seen when a personal pronoun in N2 position has to be expressed in the possessive form, for example, 'a mate of mine', not *'a mate of me'. The structure has to do with a fairly loose kind of association involving such things as common location, sponsorship, and representation, for example:

the tea shops of Japan
the Mission to the United Nations of the People's Republic of China
the closed fist salute of ZANU–PF

Modification of first noun (N1)

The previous section covers instances of *N1 of N2* which are double-headed regardless of the modification of either noun. However, an interesting process can be seen in the earlier 'focus' category where N1 is modified by one or more adjectives.

a. Japan's first taste of Western progress
b. the familiar local life of Zermatt
c. the governing mechanism of the new EEC
d. the technical resources of reconnaissance
e. a comprehensive selection of containers

Without the modifiers, we might classify **a.**, **b.**, **c.**, and **e.** under 'focus' generally, and **d.** as a support noun. It is clear that the secondary role of N1 is much enhanced by modification, so that the examples above should be regarded as double-headed. Neither N1 nor N2 can easily be omitted, because N1 is treated as a full headword. The two noun groups balance each other.

In exemplifying earlier categories, quite a few examples of modifiers of N1 were included, and these are now printed below for consideration. Many would be best placed in this double-headed category (though the semantic relation between N1 and N2 is not affected):

this first week of the war
a uniform grouping of all arms
a little shrill gasp of shock
five thousand years of superstition
a little glimmer of satisfaction
the new generation of cards

> various kinds of economic sanctions
> the familiar type of the peppery conservative
> little hope of new ideas
> some green ends of onions
> a small dried drop of it

Mopping up

It is an important feature of this method of investigation that no instances are overlooked in any sample, no matter how awkward or bizarre they might be. Those which do not readily fall into any of the preceeding categories are:

Superlative adjectives

There is clearly a regular syntactic pattern built around superlative adjectives:

> the most delectable of soups
> the most perfect fossilising medium of all

and provision must be made for it in a grammar.

Fixed phrases

In their various ways, the following seem to be relatively fixed phrases, and thus of little structural interest:

> birds of paradise
> the axis of rotation
> the patience of Job
> a court of law
> a lack of distinction

Miscellaneous

The following is an unusual example:

> fantasies of the ship's sinking.

It is probably closest to the double-headed associative relationship as in:

> the Cabinet of Dr Caligari.

Evaluation

To test the comprehensiveness and accuracy of the description, we return to the concordances to take a fresh sample of about thirty instances and see how well the classification accounts for the new evidence—see Table 1; three of these examples are used in the introduction.

The analysis of the examples in Table 1 is set out systematically with brief notes, followed by a discussion of problematic cases. The categories follow closely the sequence of the presentation above. Numbers refer to lines in Table 1.

Table 1: A Set of instances of of

1	off the end	of	Long Island
2	and you hadn't heard	of	either
3	his own degree	of	guilt
4	a small bottle	of	brandy
5	None	of	the final few clippings
6	overhung the slope	of	the Third Ice Field!
7	and would bring her some sense	of	what she was
8	the easing	of	shall we say, the rules of
9	with a touch	of	indefinable pathos in his make-up
10	with Conrad asleep in the back	of	the van,
11	a tiny little bit like the shock	of	rape
12	I think	of	the chaps on my film course
13	one has days when one isn't certain	of	anything
14	A group	of	unstable left-wing countries
15	to people who knew neither	of	them well
16	the lives of one quarter	of	the human race
17	convict these people	of	negligence, or of criminal irresponsibility
18	in the early stages	of	a conflict
19	in the midwestern states	of	North America
20	rundown buildings, modest blocks	of	flats
21	Succeeding generations	of	youthful American males
22	Operations	of	this sort
23	a series of most able incumbents	of	the post
24	it tears it open with the claws	of	its front legs
25	Dan had completed the first draft	of	his next play
26	Three hundred pounds is a lot	of	money
27	Once this sort	of	start had been made
28	was not the least	of	the sensual joys of the evening
29	spotted with the loveliest	of	colours,

| 30 | A parson's just as cunning as the rest | of | 'em when it comes to money, |

30   A parson's just as cunning as the rest   of   'em when it comes to
                                       money,
31 The patch may look newer than the rest   of   the carpet,
32   no money when you   of   all people could have had it
33   Prepare ye the way   of   the Lord
34   I found a prodigality   of   pattern and colour

Analysis of examples in Table 1

Non-nominal instances of *of*

1 phrases—none
2 verbs
   2 heard of
 12 think of
  7 convict of
3 adjectives
 13 certain of

Nominal group

1.1.1 conventional measure
   5 none of the final few
 15 neither of them
 16 one quarter of the human race
 26 a lot of money
 30 the rest of 'em
 31 the rest of the carpet

1.1.2 less conventional measures
   3 degree of guilt
   9 a touch of indefinable pathos
 14 a group of unstable left-wing countries
   4 a small bottle of brandy
 34 a prodigality of pattern and colour

1.2.1 focus on a part
   1 the end of Long Island

1.2.2 focus on a more specialized part
   6 the slope of the Third Ice Field
 10 the back of the van
 18 the early stages of a conflict
 19 states of North America

1.2.3 focus on a component, aspect, or attribute
    11 the shock of rape
    20 blocks of flats
    21 generations of youthful American males
    24 the claws of its front legs
    25 the first draft of his next play

1.3.1 support N1
    27 this sort of start
Example 7—some sense of what she was—is close enough to this category, but N2 is in this instance replaced by a clause.

1.3.2 metaphor—no examples in this sample

2.1   titles—no examples in this sample

2.2   prepositional relationships
    8 the easing of, shall we say, the rules of

3   modification of N1
The following examples are double-headed,
   e.g. 4: a small bottle of brandy
   Also: 7, 18, 19, 20, 21, 28

4.1   superlative adjectives
    29 the loveliest of colours
Note also within 28 there is another superlative:
  not the least of the sensual joys

4.2   fixed phrases
    32 you of all people
    33 Prepare ye the way of the Lord

There are two examples which do not readily fit the descriptive framework that was established in the first part of this chapter.

The following example suggests a re-ordering of type **1.3.1**, the support noun:

  22 operations of this sort

Though in this case, the support noun is at N2. Such variation looks to be quite acceptable, so this category should be redefined.

The following example looks like a propositional relationship:

  23 incumbents of the post

But no obvious equivalent sentence is possible. Since it was stressed earlier that the relationship to a clause is purely made to illustrate meaning, there is no barrier to a word like *incumbent* at N1 even though there is, by chance, no related verb.

Conclusion

The previous section demonstrates that this account of *of* is reasonably robust, and that future trawls for examples will fill out categories, but are not likely to uncover fundamentally disturbing evidence. The classification offered above forms a good basis for both a dictionary entry and a section in a grammar of English.

The ordering will probably vary: for example, it is useful in analysis to filter out uncharacteristic instances, like the non-nominal uses of *of*, but often preferable to leave them to the end in presentation.

A grammatical account will concentrate on the status of the head-word, the distinction between single and double heads, and the indeterminate cases. A dictionary might prefer to say little about this and concentrate on the classification of use.

Within the nominal group structures each version of the information will choose a level of detail depending on the space available and the intended purpose of the book. In digest form, the whole of category 1 could be summarized with two or three examples; if more space were available, the distinctions into **1.1**, **1.2**, and **1.3** would be valuable. Whether or not **1.3.2**—metaphor —is separately instanced might well be a later decision, depending on the balance of the entry.

Whatever the purpose, this study shows that a firm classification of uses and meanings can be made, despite the fact that there are some problem cases and some overlaps. For the lexicographer, there are very few usable examples in such a small selection, because each instance carries its own particularity. But a full-scale study will provide ample evidence, and among the many examples there will be some that can be cited out of context without perplexing the user.

7
Evaluating instances

Introduction

For the last four chapters, we have been studying concordances in one form or another. Each instance has been taken to be as important as any other, and has had to be accounted for. This is a valuable discipline, but only the very first step towards the automation of text study. In this chapter and the next, we begin to evaluate concordances and devise new kinds of information about language.

The starting point of this chapter is probably unexpected—it is that most actual examples are unrepresentative of the pattern of the word or phrase for which they are chosen.

Such is the intricate nature of the ties between one segment of text and the surrounding text, and the relation between the text and the world and the intended outcomes of the communication, that the act of plucking a few words from any text is not likely to provide a freestanding instance of its constituent words, each acting typically.

The vast majority can be safely discarded when their statistical contribution to the concordance as a whole has been recorded. We need a lot of text so that there will always be a sufficient residue of useful examples, and also to provide criteria for discarding the others in the first place.

Throw away your evidence

The policy of discarding examples, and particularly examples which do not fit a description, is likely to have to struggle for popularity in linguistics. The Cult of the Counter-example is still very strong, in myth if not always in observance, and it is important for students of text to define a careful position in this regard, which will be quite different from that of students of sentences. For example, the computer corpora of the early sixties, Brown (Kučera and Francis 1967) and LOB (Hofland and Johansson 1982), represent a transitional stage; they were most carefully constructed in an attempt to be representative, and each instance is cherished. The corpora are just small enough (one million words) for this to be possible for determined scholars.

The received wisdom of corpus linguistics is that fairly small corpora, of one million words or even fewer, are adequate for grammatical purposes, since the frequency of occurrence of so-called grammatical or function words is quite high. In the LOB corpus, for example (one million words of English printed in the UK in the year 1961), the commonest 100 words are almost all grammatical, and range in frequency from *the* at 68,315 to *people* at 953 (the 'lexical' words in that range are *said* 2,074, *time* 1,654, *man* 1,072, *years* 1,067). There are a few stragglers, like *shall* 348, *itself* 272, *nor* 200, *else* 169, down to *whatsoever* 7, and *whichsoever* 1; but there are numerous instances of grammatical words, sufficient to enable conventional grammatical statements to be made.

However, the availability nowadays of much larger corpora makes it possible to evaluate conventional grammatical statements. Presumably, the shorter original corpora did little more than confirm the generally agreed positions on English grammar. The new evidence suggests that grammatical generalizations do not rest on a rigid foundation, but are the accumulation of the patterns of hundreds of individual words and phrases. The language looks rather different when you look at a lot of it at once.

Such evidence has not been available before. Linguists have had to rely on their intuitions, their limited capacity for thorough textual analysis, and whatever has caught their eye or ear as they have encountered large extents of language behaviour, in their daily lives or in their professional work.

The great dictionaries of English used human beings to evaluate their examples, and there is as yet no substitute. This method is likely to highlight the unusual in English and perhaps miss some of the regular, humdrum patterns.

In grammars, the tradition of citing examples has faded away since *A Modern English Grammar* (Jespersen 1909; 1949). Even *A Comprehensive Grammar of the English Language* (CGEL) (Quirk *et al.* 1985) relies heavily on invented examples.

The CGEL had the corpus of the Survey of English Usage available to it: this is a corpus approaching one million words, spanning twenty-five years, and including a substantial proportion of spoken English.

Occasional reference is given in the grammar to Survey material, but no attempt is made to confront and account for the evidence. Hardly any of the examples are citations, though citations must have been readily available. One is forced to conclude that the authors were following a methodology which gave low priority to one of the concerns of this book, which is to press for the use of actual language data as a basis for all descriptive statements.

A valid generalization about data must relate to the data in a systematic way; each relevant instance must either support the generalization or exhibit features which make the generalization subordinate to some other descriptive statement. Hence, it is important to fix on a particular body of data (which is best chosen on non-linguistic principles), and then engage with every instance. If that procedure is adopted in language work, it soon becomes necessary to acquire very large quantities of data, or else generalizations cannot be made. Language is very complex, and people use it for their own ends, without normally being conscious of the relation between their verbal behaviour and the way that behaviour is characterized. They are creative, or expedient, or casual, or confused; or they have unusual matters to put into usual words, so they have to combine them in unusual ways.

It is, therefore, necessary to have access to a large corpus because the normal use of language is highly specific, and good representative examples are hard to find. This is as true of grammar as of lexis, because grammar is not made of just the patterns of the common grammatical words, but relies on the whole vocabulary of the language.

One further factor makes it essential to collect a large number of instances. Many words have more than one meaning, sense, or usage, and these occur in very uneven distribution. As far as I know, no systematic research has yet been done in this area, so the following remarks are speculations based on observation and occasional probings.

Frequent words have, in general, a more complex set of senses than infrequent words. If we divide and number senses in the conventional dictionary manner, we may discover a statistical relationship between the number of occurrences of a word and the number of different senses it realizes. Hence, the accumulation of instances of a frequent word is not just more of the same, but ever more clear evidence of complexity.

In addition to this, we must allow that, just as some words are much more common than others, some senses of one word are much more common than other senses of the same word—many times more common. So if we need, say, fifty occurrences of a sense of a word in order to describe it thoroughly, then the corpus has to be large enough to yield fifty instances of the least common sense. In practice, we find that the decision about the 'least common sense' is an arbitrary one; no matter what the size, there are always loose ends, unstable senses, occasional odd examples, etc. But wherever this limit is fixed, we shall observe huge discrepancies in the frequency of the recognized senses, and this will produce a heavy demand for very long texts.

Text and language

The distinction has often been made between text and language on a dimension of abstraction. Language is an abstract system; it is realized in text, which is a collection of instances. This is clearly an inadequate point of view, because we do not end up with anything like text by 'generating' word strings from grammars. In particular, there is hardly any allowance for the combinatorial meanings in text. If text (including, and in particular, spoken text) is not a strict realization of meaningful abstract decisions, then either it is subject to random distortion, or it is in part the result of decisions which are not recorded in the abstract system, but which take precedence over those which are. Many of these are components of the rather mystical notion of 'coherence' that is beyond the generative competence of grammars. Random factors will certainly not explain how coherence arises; so we are forced to conclude that the realization route is not through conventional grammars, but through some kind of functional analysis.

Actual text will always be deviant with respect to structural rules of the conventional kind. Some of the factors that lead to deviance have already been mentioned—creativity, unselfconsciousness, expediency, inattention, confusion, and the need to express the unusual. Another major factor is shared knowledge among communicators, which leads to the actual occurrence of many utterances which are proscribed by rule (for example, an obligatory transitive verb occurring without an object where the real-world thing that could give rise to an expressed object is obvious).

The grammarian's dilemma is this: does he or she study actual instances, knowing that most of them are untypical, or does he or she ignore actual instances and study a set of instances which have not

102

occurred, including a high proportion that could never occur? The former choice characterized the field linguists in the first half of this century, and the latter choice has been evident in the linguistics of the last thirty years.

The new option opened up by the computer is to evaluate actual instances and select the most typical. A complete set of typical instances should exemplify the dominant structural patterns of the language without recourse to abstraction, or indeed to generalization. The mass of instances each contain just a small element of typicality, but a few contain several typical features. In such circumstances, although it may sound paradoxical, examples which are typical are rather uncommon, and have to be found by statistical methods.

It is, therefore, unnecessary to make a sharp distinction between abstract and actual language structure—the sort of distinction embodied in Saussure's *langue* and *parole* or Chomsky's *competence* and *performance*. The existence of these dichotomies is to allow us to abstract from the chaos of life a system of meaningful choices and to insulate the abstract system. I have already conceded that some proportion of the complexity of text may be attributable to accidental or random factors, but that is far from sufficient explanation. It may indeed have obscured what actually goes on. In fact, the main simplification that is introduced by conventional grammar has nothing to do with the purity of abstraction as against the chaos of life. It is merely the decoupling of lexis and syntax.

In the explicit theoretical statement of linguistics, grammatical and lexical patterns vary independently of each other. In most grammars, it is an assumption that is obviously taken for granted. For example, it is rare for a grammar to note that a certain structure is only appropriate for a particular sense of a word. The same goes for morphology. In contrast, grammars attribute independent meaning to syntactic arrangements.

Equally, it is rare for a dictionary to note the common syntactic patterns of a word in a particular sense. Pedagogical dictionaries are increasingly seeing this as essential information for learners, but it is added in the form of afterthoughts such as usage notes. The implicit stance of a conventional dictionary entry is that most of the words in daily use have several meanings, and any occurrence of the word could signal any one of the meanings. If this were actually the case, communication would be virtually impossible.

The decoupling of lexis and syntax leads to the creation of a rubbish dump that is called 'idiom', 'phraseology', 'collocation', and the like. If two systems are held to vary independently of each other, then any instances of one constraining the other will be consigned to a limbo for odd features, occasional observations, usage notes, etc. But if evidence accumulates to suggest that a substantial proportion of the language description is of this mixed nature, then the original decoupling must be called into question. The evidence now becoming available casts grave doubts on the wisdom of postulating separate domains of lexis and syntax.

In modern lexical research, it is part of the long-term task to specify accurately the established phrases of a language. A phrase can be defined for the moment as a co-occurrence of words which creates a sense that is not the simple combination of the sense of each of the words. One is first struck by the fixity and regularity of phrases, then by their flexibility and variability, then by the characteristically creative extensions and adaptations which occur, sometimes more often than the 'ordinary' form.

In this work, it is much more fruitful to start by supposing that lexical and syntactic choices correlate, than that they vary independently of each other.

Meaning and structure

For the remainder of this chapter (as in Chapter 4), I should like to widen the domain of syntax to include lexical structure as well, and call the broader domain *structure*. In the spirit of the preceding argument, I shall define structure as any privileges of occurrence of morphemes; we do not in the first analysis have to decide whether these are lexical or syntactic—or as so often—a bit of both.

Is it then best to hypothesize that sense and structure are inseparable? Unfortunately not. If that were so, ambiguity would be impossible. More than one sense can be realized by the same structure, and, in the simplest case, by the same word.

We must, then, consider whether ambiguity is incidental or systematic. If it is much more than incidental and occasional, then it will constitute strong evidence for the independence of lexis and syntax. However, although ambiguity causes great headaches in automatic parsing, if we look at the way people actually operate with language we see it as a sporadic and almost accidental coincidence of realization, rarely constituting a communicative problem. Much more of it would threaten the basic notion of realization in language—that structure realizes sense and therefore normally differentiates one sense from another.

If sense and structure are not independent of each other and not inseparable, then they must be associated. Here we can frame a hypothesis that can act as a substitute for the langue/parole distinction. We can postulate that the underlying unit of composition is an integrated sense–structure complex, but that the exigencies of text frequently obscure this. This position offers a sharp contrast to the atomistic model featured by most grammars, and the argument is developed in the next chapter.

Our descriptive task then becomes the identification of the regular and typical associations, leading to the identification of one or more 'citation forms' for each distinct sense. The distinguishing features of the citation forms could then be stated, and explanations could be offered for the occurrence of non-citation forms. A citation form would involve a modest step in abstraction. It is also likely that many citation forms contain some systematic variables, such as pronoun selections, which leaves a modicum of independence to the grammar.

Procedure

How, then, do we find the citation forms, especially since we believe text to be largely composed of non-citation forms? I propose to outline a method for tackling one area of structure, in this case collocation, which gives promise of valuable results. The same principle can be applied to other structural features.

The procedure begins with a machine-generated concordance to a large corpus, as we have used in previous studies in this book. The usual kind of concordance is adequate, where all the occurrences of a word-form are retrieved, each in the middle of a line of text. A line of text may contain as many as eight or nine words on either side of the central word, or *node*, and we do not expect to need more than four or five on either side.

A concordance has many of the properties of a natural text, and it is reasonable for the purposes of statistical analysis to treat each cited line as if it were a sentence, and so to examine the vocabulary of the concordance. In order to do this, a list is compiled in frequency order, of all the word-forms in the concordance. These are called the *collocates* of the node. This raw list is then processed as follows:

a. The lines are trimmed so that only those words that are reasonably likely to be attracted by the node are left in. It was strongly suggested in Sinclair, Jones, and Daley (1970) that beyond four words from the node there were no statistical indications of the attractive power of the node. At present we are experimenting with environments of between one and five words on either side of the node, both balanced and unbalanced, to see if there is an optimum setting.

b. There is no point in considering very infrequent collocates, and there is usually a long tail to the frequency lists. A suitable cut-off point—for example, less than ten per cent of the frequency of the node—should be determined.

c. Each of the remaining collocates is given a weighting by relating its frequency in the concordance to its overall frequency in the full corpus. So a common word gets a low rating, and a word which makes a distinctive collocation with the node will score high.

d. Each line of the concordance is now examined for the typicality of its collocates, by adding up the weightings of each collocate in its environment. The concordance is now re-sorted into an order of typicality, and the most typical instances should come to the top.

From this point onwards, an automatic procedure is not yet fully established, and the study continues largely on a subjective basis. First, any obvious phrases are identified and removed. Next, there is a search for the clustering of collocates and their mutual attraction and repulsion, for example, pairs and groups of collocates which frequently occur in the same line, and pairs which never do. Then the other aspects of structural patterning are brought in—the occurrence of the very frequent words, syntactic structures, ordering of items in the line, and so on.

If it is suspected that there are two or more principal senses of a word, an attempt is made to isolate a sense, using explicit criteria. When a sense is fully described, all the lines that exemplify it are then removed, and the new, shorter concordance is reprocessed from the beginning.

Gradually, this procedure should identify the distinct senses of a word. Each cycle will, however, reduce the size of the remaining concordance substantially, and the overall size of the corpus will quickly become a limiting factor.

Findings

This technique, in a provisional form, was recently applied to the concordance of the word *second*. The word was chosen as being fairly frequent (over 1,200 occurrences in 7.3 million), and as having two rather distinctive major senses. It was found that the first pass identified *the Second World War* as a phrase which had 14 occurrences in the 50 most typical. The next pass, omitting the 14 phrases, identified a major sense which was strongly associated with preceding *the*, occasionally *his* or *her*, and with words like *first, third, time, year, act, child,* and *wife* in the environment. The next pass identified a sense which was strongly associated with preceding *per*, and before that a word like *cycles, radians*. A number of similar instances had *a* instead of *per* but *a* is also occasionally used in the other main sense.

There was little else except a hint of possible phrases *second hand* and *second class*.

The two main meanings of *second*, then, are associated one with definiteness and the other with indefiniteness. This is at least as important as the observation that one is a modifier and one a noun.

A closer look at the full concordance confirms these findings. There is, however, a third fairly prominent use of *second* which does not emerge in the collocational analysis. This requires neither a definite nor an indefinite determiner, and the word functions as a discourse organizer. It is quite often preceded by *and*. It is not surprising that this use does not attract strong lexical collocations, because it occurs according to the exigencies of the discourse and should be largely independent of such things as content, topic, message.

These findings are crude, preliminary, and partial. No doubt a study of *secondly* would identify the third sense of *second* as a discourse organizer to be absorbed into the lemma *second(ly)*. The study of *seconds* might add new features and new uses, and so on. In due course, we shall see. The technique has at least managed to isolate the most basic contrast of meaning. In another trial at an international conference in 1988, the prototype system successfully distinguished among *sole* = only, *sole* = fish, and *sole* = bottom of shoes or feet.

Conclusion

The conclusion that can be drawn from this and other examples is that it is folly to decouple lexis and syntax, or either of those and semantics. The realization of meaning is much more explicit than is suggested by abstract grammars. The model of a highly generalized formal syntax, with slots into which fall neat lists of words, is suitable only in rare uses and specialized texts. By far the majority of text is made of the occurrence of common words in common patterns, or in slight variants of those common patterns. Most everyday words do not have an independent meaning, or meanings, but are components of a rich repertoire of multi-word patterns that make up text. This is totally obscured by the procedures of conventional grammar.

The next chapter takes up this argument in detail. The notion of citation forms is developed in a separate publication (Sinclair 1984).

8
Collocation

Introduction

This chapter concludes the description of word co-occurrence as we currently conceive it. The next stage is to write a dictionary of collocations, and the project is in hand (Sinclair *et al.* forthcoming). The argument brings together a number of themes that have been developing throughout the book, in particular, the notions of dependent and independent meaning, and the relation of texts to grammar.

Two models of interpretation

It is contended here that in order to explain the way in which meaning arises from language text, we have to advance two different principles of interpretation. One is not enough. No single principle has been advanced which accounts for the evidence in a satisfactory way. The two principles are.

The open-choice principle ✗

This is a way of seeing language text as the result of a very large number of complex choices. At each point where a unit is completed (a word or a phrase or a clause), a large range of choice opens up and the only restraint is grammaticalness.

This is probably the normal way of seeing and describing language. It is often called a 'slot-and-filler' model, evisaging texts as a series of slots which have to be filled from a lexicon which satisifies local restraints. At each slot, virtually any word can occur. Since language is believed to operate simultaneously on several levels, there is a very complex pattern of choices in progress at any moment, but the underlying principle is simple enough.

Any segmental approach to description which deals with progressive choices is of this type. Any tree structure shows it clearly: the nodes on the tree are the choice points. Virtually all grammars are constructed on the open-choice principle.

The idiom principle

It is clear that words do not occur at random in a text, and that the open-choice principle does not provide for substantial enough restraints on consecutive choices. We would not produce normal text simply by operating the open-choice principle.

To some extent, the nature of the world around us is reflected in the organization of language and contributes to the unrandomness. Things which occur physically together have a stronger chance of being mentioned together; also concepts in the same philosophical area, and the results of exercising a number of organizing features such as contrasts or series. But even allowing for these, there are many ways of saying things, many choices within language that have little or nothing to do with the world outside.

There are sets of linguistic choices which come under the heading of register, and which can be seen as large-scale conditioning choices. Once a register choice is made, and these are normally social choices, then all the slot-by-slot choices are massively reduced in scope or even, in some cases, pre-empted.

Allowing for register as well, there is still far too much opportunity for choice in the model, and the principle of idiom is put forward to account for the restraints that are not captured by the open-choice model.

The principle of idiom is that a language user has available to him or her a large number of semi-preconstructed phrases that constitute single choices, even though they might appear to be analysable into segments. To some extent, this may reflect the recurrence of similar situations in human affairs; it may illustrate a natural tendency to economy of effort; or it may be motivated in part by the exigencies of real-time conversation. However it arises, it has been relegated to an inferior position in most current linguistics, because it does not fit the open-choice model.

At its simplest, the principle of idiom can be seen in the apparently simultaneous choice of two words, for example, *of course*. This phrase operates effectively as a single word, and the word space, which is structurally bogus, may disappear in time, as we see in *maybe, anyway,* and *another*.

Where there is no variation in the phrase, we are dealing with a fairly trivial mismatch between the writing system and the grammar. The *of* in *of course* is not the preposition *of* that is found in grammar books. The preposition *of* is normally found after the noun head of a nominal group, or in a quantifier like *a pint of* ... . In an open-choice model, *of* can be followed by any nominal group (see Chapter 6 for details). Similarly, *course* is not the countable noun that dictionaries mention; its meaning is not a property of the word, but of the phrase. If it were a countable noun in the singular it would have to be preceded by a determiner to be grammatical, so it clearly is not.

It would be reasonable to add phrases like *of course* to the list of compounds, like *cupboard*, whose elements have lost their semantic identity, and make allowance for the intrusive word space. The same treatment could be given to hundreds of similar phrases—any occasion where one decision leads to more than one word in text. Idioms, proverbs, clichés, technical terms, jargon expressions, phrasal verbs, and the like could all be covered by a fairly simple statement.

However, the principle of idiom is far more pervasive and elusive than we have allowed so far. It has been noted by many writers on language, but its importance has been largely neglected. Some features of the idiom principle follow:

a. Many phrases have an indeterminate extent. As an example, consider *set eyes on*. This seems to attract a pronoun subject, and either *never* or a temporal conjunction like *the moment, the first time*, and the word *has* as an auxiliary to *set*. How much of this is integral to the phrase, and how much is in the nature of collocational attraction?

b. Many phrases allow internal lexical variation. For example, there seems to be little to choose between *in some cases* and *in some instances*; or between *set x on fire* and *set fire to x*.

c. Many phrases allow internal lexical syntactic variation. Consider the phrase *it's not in his nature to* ... . The word *it* is part of the phrase, and so is the verb *is*—though this verb can vary to *was* and perhaps can include modals. *Not* can be replaced by any 'broad' negative, including *hardly, scarcely,* etc. *In* is fixed, but *his* can be replaced by any possessive pronoun and perhaps by some names with *'s*. *Nature* is fixed.

d. Many phrases allow some variation in word order. Continuing the last example, we can postulate *to recriminate is not in his nature,* or *it is not in the nature of an academic to* ... .

111

e. Many uses of words and phrases attract other words in strong collocation; for example, *hard work, hard luck, hard facts, hard evidence.*

f. Many uses of words and phrases show a tendency to co-occur with certain grammatical choices. For example, it was pointed out in Chapter 5 that the phrasal verb *set about*, in its meaning of something like 'inaugurate', is closely associated with a following verb in the *-ing* form, for example, *set about leaving* ... . What is more, the second verb is usually transitive, for example, *set about testing it.* Very often, *set* will be found in co-occurrence patterns.

g. Many uses of words and phrases show a tendency to occur in a certain semantic environment. For example, the verb *happen* is associated with unpleasant things—accidents and the like.

The overwhelming nature of this evidence leads us to elevate the principle of idiom from being a rather minor feature, compared with grammar, to being at least as important as grammar in the explanation of how meaning arises in text. Support comes unexpectedly from a different quarter.

Evidence from long texts

In the current lexical analysis of long texts, a number of problems have arisen, not all of which were anticipated:

1 The 'meanings' of very frequent, so-called grammatical words are a headache in any lexicography, but the problem they typify fits in with some of the newer difficulties.

2 Some 'meanings' of frequent words seem to have very little meaning at all, for example, *take*, in *take a look at this*; *make* in *make up your mind*.

3 The commonest meanings of the commonest words are not the meanings supplied by introspection; for example, the meaning of *back* as 'the posterior part of the human body, extending from the neck to the pelvis' (*Collins English Dictionary* (*CED*) 2nd edition 1986 sense 1) is not a very common meaning. Not until sense 47, the second adverbial sense, do we come to 'in, to or towards the original starting point, place or condition', which is closer to the commonest usage in our evidence.

I think most speakers of English would agree with the *CED*'s ordering of senses, whatever the evidence from frequency. What is disquieting is the apparent lack of good reason for the enormous discrepancy between the sense to which our intuitions give priority, and the most frequent one.

4 The commonest meanings of many less common words are not those supplied by introspection. Sense 1 offered in the *CED* for *pursue* is 'to follow (a fugitive etc.) in order to capture or overtake', yet by far the commonest meaning is sense 5, 'to apply oneself to (one's studies, hobbies, interests etc.)'.

From this evidence, we can put forward some tentative generalizations:

1 There is a broad general tendency for frequent words, or frequent senses of words, to have less of a clear and independent meaning than less frequent words or senses. These meanings of frequent words are difficult to identify and explain; and, with the very frequent words, we are reduced to talking about uses rather than meanings. The tendency can be seen as a progressive delexicalization, or reduction of the distinctive contribution made by that word to the meaning.

2 This dependency of meaning correlates with the operation of the idiom principle to make fewer and larger choices. The evidence of collocation supports the point. If the words collocate significantly, then to the extent of that significance, their presence is the result of a single choice.

3 The 'core' meaning of a word—the one that first comes to mind for most people—will not normally be a delexical one. A likely hypothesis is that the 'core' meaning is the most frequent independent sense. This hypothesis would have to be extensively tested, but if it proved to hold good then it would help to explain the discrepancy referred to above between the most frequent sense and what intuition suggests is the most important or central one.

4 Most normal text is made up of the occurrence of frequent words, and the frequent senses of less frequent words. Hence, normal text is largely delexicalized, and appears to be formed by exercise of the idiom principle, with occasional switching to the open-choice principle.

5 Just as it is misleading and unrevealing to subject *of course* to grammatical analysis, it is also unhelpful to attempt to analyse grammatically any portion of text which appears to be constructed on the idiom principle.

113

The last point contains an implication that a description must indicate how users know which way to interpret each portion of an utterance. The boundaries between stretches constructed on different principles will not normally be clear-cut, and not all stretches carry as much evidence as *of course* does to suggest that it is not constructed by the normal rules of grammar.

It should be recognized that the two models of language that are in use are incompatible with each other. There is no shading of one into another; the switch from one model to the other will be sharp. The models are diametrically opposed.

The last two points taken together suggest one reason why language text is often indeterminate in its interpretation and hence very flexible in use. If the 'switch points' between two modes of intepretation are not always explicitly signalled, and the two modes offer sharply contrasting ways of interpreting the data, then it is quite likely that an utterance will not be interpreted in exactly the same way in which it was constructed. Also, two listeners, or two readers, will not interpret in precisely the same way.

For normal texts, we can put forward the proposal that the first mode to be applied is the idiom principle, since most of the text will be interpretable by this principle. Whenever there is good reason, the interpretive process switches to the open-choice principle, and quickly back again. Lexical choices which are unexpected in their environment will presumably occasion a switch; choices which, if grammatically interpreted, would be unusual are an affirmation of the operation of the idiom principle.

Some texts may be composed in a tradition which makes greater than normal use of the open-choice principle; legal statements, for example. Some poems may contrast the two principles of interpretation. But these are specialized genres that require additional practice in understanding.

It thus appears that a model of language which divides grammar and lexis, and which uses the grammar to provide a string of lexical choice points, is a secondary model. It cannot be relinquished, because a text still has many switch points where the open-choice model will come into play. It has an abstract relevance, in the sense that much of the text shows a potential for being analysed as the result of open choices, but the other principle, the idiom principle, dominates. The open-choice analysis could be imagined as an analytical process which goes on in principle all the time, but whose results are only intermittently called for.

114

This view of how the two principles are deployed in interpretation can be used to make predictions about the way people behave, and the accuracy of the predictions can be used as a measure of the accuracy of the model. Areas of relevant study include: the transitional probabilities of words; the prevalent notion of *chunking* (see Chapter 9); the occurrence of hesitations, etc., and the placement of boundaries; and the behaviour of subjects trying to guess the next word in a mystery text.

Collocation

The above is the framework within which I would like to consider the role of collocation. Collocation, as has been mentioned, illustrates the idiom principle. On some occasions, words appear to be chosen in pairs or groups and these are not necessarily adjacent.

One aspect of collocation has been of enduring interest. When two words of different frequencies collocate significantly, the collocation has a different value in the description of each of the two words. If word *a* is twice as frequent as word *b*, then each time they occur together is twice as important for *b* than it is for *a*. This is because that particular event accounts for twice the proportion of the occurrence of *b* than of *a*.

So when all the occurrences of *a* with *b* are counted up and evaluated, one figure is recorded in the profile of *a*, and another figure double the size, is recorded in the profile of *b*.

By entering the same set of events twice, once as the collocation of *a* with *b* and again as the collocation of *b* with *a*, one incurs the strictures of Benson, Brainerd, and Greaves (1985) who say 'there are two problems here: double counting of nodes and double counting of collocates. The parts now add up to considerably more than the whole, which makes computation under any statistical model inaccurate'. In practice, the possibility of double entry allows us to highlight two different aspects of collocation.

I would like to consider separately the two types of collocation instanced above, using the term *node* for the word that is being studied, and the term *collocate* for any word that occurs in the specified environment of a node. Each successive word in a text is thus both node and collocate, though never at the same time.

When *a* is node and *b* is collocate, I shall call this *downward collocation*—collocation of *a* with a less frequent word (*b*). When *b* is node and *a* is collocate, I shall call this *upward collocation*. The whole of a given word list may be treated in this way.

There appears to be a systematic difference between upward and downward collocation. Upward collocation, of course, is the weaker pattern in statistical terms, and the words tend to be elements of grammatical frames, or superordinates. Downward collocation by contrast gives us a semantic analysis of a word.

Collocation of *back*

Let us illustrate collocational patterns, in a provisional way, with the word *back*. I shall make no attempt to differentiate separate senses, but will put the collocates into *ad hoc* groups.

No standard of statistical significance is claimed at present, because many typical collocations are of such low frequency compared with the overall length of a text. Because of the low frequency of the vast majority of words, almost any repeated collocation is a most unlikely event, but because the set of texts is so large, unlikely events of this kind may still be the result of chance factors.

However, no speaker of English would doubt the importance of these patterns. One recognizes them immediately, because they are features of the organization of texts; often subliminal, they cannot be reliably retrieved by introspection.

In distinguishing upward and downward collocation I have made a buffer area of (plus or minus) 15 per cent of the frequency of the node word. For example, let us take a word occurring 1,000 times; when it is examined as a node, collocates are grouped into:

a. upward collocates—those whose own occurrence is over 115 per cent of the node frequency (that is, 1,150);
b. neutral collocates—between 85 per cent and 115 per cent of the node frequency (in this instance, 850 and 1,150), this is the buffer area;
c. downward collocates—less than 80 per cent (in this instance, 850).

Neutral collocates are added on an *ad hoc* basis to upward or downward groups, and are given round brackets. Since this has to be a summary account of a very large set of data, I have removed some items which seem to be of little general significance. These include personal names, contracted forms like *I'll*, and word-forms whose

116

co-occurrence with *back* is infrequent and carries no conviction of any general significance. Of the last category, the form *anger* only occurs in the title of the play *Look Back in Anger*.

The nouns and verbs listed below as collocating with *back* are representative only. Given the uncertainty at the limits of statistical significance, it could be more misleading to include doubtful contenders. Thus, while *get, go*, and *bring* are unlikely to be challenged, *beach, box*, and *bus* are much less convincing when the actual instances are examined.

The qualification for an instance being scrutinized is co-occurrence within four words of *back*, on either side, this being the cut-off point established some years ago (Jones and Sinclair 1974). No account is taken of syntax, punctuation, change of speaker, or anything other than the word-forms themselves.

No doubt the studies which succeed this one will sharpen up the picture considerably. For example, the evidence of *back* suggests that few intuitively interesting collocations cross a punctuation mark. But it would be unwise to generalize from the pattern of one word, particularly such an unusual one as *back*. Now that tagged and parsed texts are becoming available, the co-patterning of lexical and grammatical choices is open to research. But it is still important to draw attention to the strength of patterning which emerges from the rawest of unprocessed data.

In pushing forward into new kinds of observation of language, the computer is simultaneously pulling us back to some very basic facts that are often ignored in linguistics. The set of four choices, a,b,c,k, from the alphabet, arranged in the sequence b,a,c,k with nothing in between them, that is, *back*, is an important linguistic event in its own right, long before it is ascribed a word-class or a meaning. It is difficult for users of English to notice this, but it is the computer's starting point.

Analysis of the collocational pattern of *back*

Upward collocates: back

Prepositions/adverbs/conjunctions: *at, (down), from, into, now, on, then, to, up, when*

Pronouns: *her, him, me, she, them, we*

Possessive pronouns: *her, his, my, (your)*

Verb: *get, (go), got*

The meaning of *back* as 'return' attracts expressions of time and place; *after* and *where* are also prominent. The presence of four subject pronouns may have a more general explanation than anything to do with *back*, but the absence of *you* and *I* from the list may be worth pursuing. Possessive pronouns suggest the anatomical sense of *back* and would explain why *they* and *their* do not figure prominently. The two verbs *get* and *go* are superordinates of a large number of verbs of motion, many of which will be found in the downward collocates.

I have selected a few examples of these words to show the way in which the basic syntax of *back* is established. The sets of examples follow the four categories mentioned above:

It really was like being back *at* school
He drive back *down* to the terrace
When our parents came back *from* Paris
I followed him back *into* the wood
A hefty slap *on* the back

He turned back to the bookshelf
When can I have *him* back home, doctor?
She went back to her typing
It would be nice to have *them* back
We went back to the bungalow

She has gone back to *her* parents
He want back into *his* office
I ran back to *my* cabin
Go back to *your* dormitory at once

Now I must *get* back to work
They *go* back to the same nest

Downward collocates: back

Verbs: *arrive, bring, etc., climbed, come, etc., cut, etc., dates, etc., drew, etc., drove, etc., fall, etc., flew, flung, handed, hold, etc., jerked, lay, etc., leaned, etc., looked, looking, etc., pay, pulled, etc., pushed, etc., put, ran, rocking, rolled, rush, sank, sat, etc., sent, etc., shouted, snapped, stared, stepped, steps, etc., stood, threw, traced, turned, etc., walked, etc., waved.*

Prepositions: *along, behind, onto, past, toward, towards*

Adverbs: *again, forth, further, slowly, straight*

Adjective: *normal*

Nouns: *camp, flat, garden, home, hotel, office, road, streets, village, yard*
bed, chair, couch, door, sofa, wall, window, feet, forehead, hair, hand, head, neck, shoulder, car, seat
mind, sleep,
kitchen, living room, porch, room.

The word-class groupings above are based on frequency with *back*; many words actually occur in more than one word-class. Verbs are given in their most frequent form. Note the preponderance of past tense verbs, reflecting the temporal meaning of *back*.

The prepositions and adverbs suggest some typical phrases with *back*, and the nouns are largely those of direction, physical space, and human anatomy. A few typical examples follow:

Verbs: You *arrive* back on the Thursday
    May *bring* it back into fashion
    We *climbed* back up on the stepladder
    They had *come* back to England
    She never *cut* back on flowers
    It possibly *dates* back to the war
    The bearer *drew* back in fear
    We *drove* back to Cambridge
    You can *fall* back on something definite
    I *flew* back home in a light aircraft
    He *flung* back the drapes joyously
    Don't try to *hold* her back
    She *lay* back in the darkness
    He *leaned* back in his chair
    He *looked* back at her, and their eyes met
    Pay me back for all you took from me
    Pulled back the bedclothes and climbed into bed
    I *pushed* back my chair and made to rise
    Shall I *put* it back in the box for you
    I *rolled* back onto the grass
    She *sat* back and crossed her legs
    Edward was *sent* back to school
    He *shouted* back
    The girl *stared* back
    They *started* walking back to Fifth Avenue

He *stepped* back and said ...
He then *stood* back for a minute
The woman *threw* her head back
These could be *traced* back to the early sixties
He *turned* back to the bookshelf
She *walked* back to the bus stop
We *waved* back like anything

Prepositions: Hands held *behind* his back
Walked back *toward* the house

Adverbs: Later we came back *again*
Rock us gently back and *forth*
If you look *further* back in my files
The *straight* back to his cabin
He went *slowly* back to his book

Adjective: Things would soon get back to *normal*

Nouns: I crawled back to *camp*
I'll drive you back to your *flat*
Not a bit like his back *garden*
He turned and went back *home*
We had to go back to the *hotel*
You've just got back from the *office*
Set back from the *road*
The back *streets* of Glasgow
All the way back to the *village*
On his *way* back to the apartment
Without even a back *yard*
Go back to *bed*
He leaned back in his *chair*
Stepping outside the back *door*
A man standing by the back *wall*
Tom went back to the *window*
Britain would be back on its *feet*
He brushed back his *hair*
With the back of his *hand*
She put her *head* back against the seat
The hairs on the back of my *neck*
He gestured back over his *shoulder*
They got back into the *car*

120

There was some beer on the back *seat*
In the back of his *mind*
Then we go back to *sleep* again
You must come back to the *kitchen*
She went back into the *living room*
Beside me here on the back *porch*
He came back into the *room*

Conclusion

All the evidence points to an underlying rigidity of phraseology, despite a rich superficial variation. Hardly any collocates occur more than once in more than two patterns. The phraseology is frequently discriminatory in terms of sense; for example, there are almost as many instances of *flat on her back* as *back to her flat*. Some, like *arrive*, seem characteristic of the spoken language, some, like *hotel*, show the wisdom of allowing a nine-word span for collocation.

Early predictions of lexical structure were suitably cautious; there was no reason to believe that the patterns of lexis should map on to semantic structures. For one thing, lexis was syntagmatic and semantics was paradigmatic; for another, lexis was limited to evidence of physical co-occurrence, whereas semantics was intuitive and associative.

The early results given here are characteristic of present evidence; there is a great deal of overlap with semantics, and very little reason to posit an independent semantics for the purpose of text description.

9

Words about words

Introduction

In the final chapter, we look at the way in which people explain the meaning of words, especially in dictionaries. Although lexicography is a practical skill, a dictionary is a systematic description of a language. In turn, it must be assumed that any such description rests on the foundations of a theoretical position, whether articulated or not.

The argument in this chapter makes something of a contrast with that in earlier work (Sinclair 1984), where I make a case against the attempt to devise a theory of lexicography. At that time, lexicography seemed to me to be almost entirely a matter of managing a number of routine factors like resources and project aims. The relevant theory was linguistic theory, pure and simple. Expertise in computation, printing, book design, reference, and other skills was required from time to time, but this was not felt to be of a theoretical nature, even when, as in computational science, theory was readily available. Lexicography was held up by the practitioners to be a largely practical matter, and theories got in the way.

However, in the later stages of compiling the Cobuild dictionary (Sinclair *et al.* 1987) it was decided to develop a new style of presenting lexicographical information. The process began in a straightforward attempt to explain the meaning and use of words in ordinary English sentences, and it ended in a radical critique of conventional lexicography. This exercise now appears to be the first step in articulating a theory of language reflexivity—the capacity of language to talk about itself. The importance of this capacity has not been properly recognized as yet, or even the extent of its occurrence in everyday usage. This chapter hopes to contribute to a better understanding of language about language.

The rationale is set out in Hanks (1987). Each entry for a word in the Cobuild dictionary begins with some formal matters like a listing of word-forms, and a guide to pronunciation. Then, paragraph by paragraph, the meanings and uses of the word are explained. At the end of each explanation there is usually an example. To the side of the main text is an extra column with abbreviated notes on grammar and semantics.

In this chapter, I shall concentrate on the structure of explanations. The explanations lead to hypotheses about inference, metalanguage, and the general nature of lexical statement.

Here are some representative lexical statements from the Cobuild dictionary:

A **house** is a building in which people live ...
If you **defeat** someone, you win a victory over them in a contest such as a battle, game or argument.
A **pure** substance is not mixed with anything else.
If something happens **often**, it happens many times or much of the time.

Structure

These statements are first of all divisible into two principal parts:

A **house**	is a building in which people live ...
If you **defeat** someone	you win a victory over them in a contest ...
A **pure** substance	is not mixed with anything else.
If something happens **often**	it happens many times or much of the time.

The first parts of each sentence break down further into two sub-parts, shown by the type-face changes. One or more words are in bold type, and the rest is in roman. The word or phrase in bold type is called the *topic* of the sentence, and the rest of the first part can be called the *co-text*. For example, in the second statement above, *defeat* is the topic, and *if you* and *someone* constitute the co-text.

The second part of each sentence is an explanatory comment on the topic, and is called the *comment*. Comments are sometimes divisible according to the surface syntax. This is called *chunking*; in this kind of sentence, successive chunks express gradually increasing depth of detail.

There is another element of structure in each of the statements, and it can occur physically in either the first part or the second part. This element is an indication of the actual sentence structure, and is called the *operator*. In the statements above, the operators are:

a. the outset of the first part: *if*;
b. at the outset of the second part: *is*.

Table 1 shows the analysis so far:

124

FIRST PART				SECOND PART		CHUNKS
OPERATOR	CO-TEXT (1)	TOPIC	CO-TEXT (2)	OPERATOR	COMMENT	
	a	house		is	a building	1
					in which people live	2
if	you	defeat	someone		you win a victory over them	1
					in a contest such as …	2
	a	pure	substance	is	not mixed wit anything else	
if	something happens	often			it happens many times	1
					or much of the time	2

Table 1: Primary structure of lexical statement

Variation in co-text

There are some types of the first part that are quite different from those presented so far.

About the word itself

The statement may be about the word itself, and may not use the device of putting the word as topic in an appropriate context, for example:

You use **naturally** to indicate that you think something is very obvious.

In ordinary written English, the word *naturally* in the above example would be highlighted in some way—italics or inverted commas usually. Since it is a dictionary headword and in bold face, it is not further distinguished. However, this type of sentence is a different way of tackling the job of explanation. Other examples are:

Naturalistic describes people or things that ...
Meanwhile means while a particular thing is happening.
To **levitate** means to rise and float in the air.
To **torture** someone means ...

What people mean

The statement may be about what people mean when they use a word or phrase, rather than what the word or phrase means:

If you describe a woman as a **cow** ...
If you say that something **gets up** your nose ...
If you say that something is **smashing**, you ...
If you refer to someone as a **pipsqueak**, you ...

In these cases, it is important to point out that the opinion of the speaker is crucial to correct usage. Nothing is inherently 'smashing', in the way that it might be 'smooth' or 'strong'. The co-text includes a verb such as *describe, say, refer, call*, and the topic is found in a subordinate clause or a similar secondary structure. This strategy is part of the 'report' category in grammar, and typically a report contains a statement inside it.

Hence, in: 'If you describe a woman as a **cow** ...' you are reported as saying that the woman is a cow. *That woman is a cow* is close in structure to *a house is a building*, which is a structure already analysed. The new structure including report can be represented as follows in Table 2:

First Part				
OPERATOR	CO-TEXT			TOPIC
	REPORT	'topic'	'operator'	'comment'
If	you describe	a woman	as a	**cow ...**

Table 2: Report structures

The other examples can be described in similar ways. The terms *topic, operator,* and *comment* are re-used but in lower case and inside inverted commas to make it clear that they are embedded. Note that the comment at the lower level is the topic at the text level.

The Cobuild dictionary is sparing with explanations of this type, and only uses them when it would be misleading to ignore the subjective quality of the meaning. For example, it was implied above that 'smooth' and 'strong' were inherent qualities, but on closer inspection they are seen to be quite subjective. Something is smooth only if there is general agreement about that as a description of it. Some objective qualities of the object referred to will be relevant in deciding whether or not it can be called smooth. In contrast, if you consider something or someone 'smashing', that seems to be a very personal judgement.

Structure: verb explanations

Animate subjects

I return to the normal type of entry, to consider further the structure of the co-text. The focus is on the explanation of verbs.

In nearly every entry there is reference to a person; the sort of person who will be using English. The neutral way of referring to this person is with the pronoun *you*, and in this sense it is used many times on each page of the Cobuild dictionary.

Occasionally, though, *you* is felt not to be appropriate. The implication of using *you* is that the sentence expresses something that anyone might reasonably and normally do, so when we are explaining things which are socially undesirable, the pronoun *you* may be replaced by *someone*, for example:

If someone **burps**, they make a noise ...
If someone **totters**, they walk in an unsteady way ...
If someone **flings** you into prison, ...

If someone **defrauds** you, ...
If someone **burgles** a building, ...

Notice that *you* sometimes reappears as the object of the verb, so that the co-text presents the action as something happening to a person who may be the user, rather than the other way round.

There is a lot of room here for interpretation of what is taken to be socially undesirable, and the dictionary projects an evaluative view of the world through devices of this nature.

At present the use of *someone* as both subject and object is avoided, so **seduce** begins 'If you seduce someone', rather than 'If someone seduces someone'. The third possibility, 'If someone seduces you', carries an implication of this being a reasonably probable event, and so is avoided.

Someone also replaces *you* if the sentence expresses an activity which is difficult, unusual, or outside the subject's control, for example:

If someone **slips** into a particular state or activity, they change into it ...
When someone **drowns**, ...
When someone **sews**, ...
If someone **tames** a wild animal or bird, ...

Where an activity is so undesirable or unusual that it would sound absurd to suggest that ordinary people do it, the choice of a subject is abandoned altogether. Instead, the explanation takes the form of a statement about the word itself, as instanced earlier in the section on 'Variation in co-text':

To **levitate** means to rise and float in the air ...
To **torture** someone means ...

An occasional alternative to *someone* is the word *people*, which is plural and so is more natural in the description of communal activities:

When people **ski**, ...
If people **riot**, ...
When people **demonstrate**, ...
If people **agree** on something, ...

The use of words like *someone* and *people* allows an important development of the co-text which is denied to the word *you*. One of the problems of explaining usage is how to decide which of these alternatives applies to each new word.

The words *someone* and *people* can be qualified by adding an illustrative or restrictive phrase:

If someone who is very ill is **sinking**, ...
If someone, especially a child, **sneaks** on you, ...
If someone in authority **rules** on a particular situation or problem ...

It is a small step from that to name directly a suitable subject for the topic verb:

If the police **arrest** you, ...
When artists **exhibit** ...

The disadvantage of this last structure is that it appears by a natural sort of implication to exclude anyone other than the named people. It is thus a risky statement to make in a dictionary because the conventions of language are so easily extended. On the other hand, it is clumsy and uneconomical to keep saying 'If someone such as a policeman arrests you ...', when the likelihood of being arrested by anyone else is very small.

We must presume, then, that in the cases of direct naming it is unlikely, but not impossible, that someone other than the named person may be an appropriate subject.

Playing is associated particularly with children, and also with pet animals. Adults do it occasionally, but their play is more often expressed in clauses with an object, for example, 'Do you play chess?'. The entry in Cobuild opens thus:

When children, animals or perhaps adults **play**,

Similarly, the entry for **sting** begins:

If an insect, animal, or plant **stings** you, ...

The creatures that cause a sting are partially identified. Similarly, the entry for **lay** includes the sense:

When a bird or female animal **lays** an egg ...

The conventions of interpretation apply to non-humans in the same way as to humans, and to mixtures of human and non-human. For example, it would not be sufficiently specific to present the verb *play* in the co-text 'when you *play* ...' or even 'when people *play* ...'.

Inanimate subjects

Inanimate objects and abstract entities are dealt with by a similar set of conventions based on the word *something*. Here are some examples:

> If something **glows**, ...
> If something **ensues**, ...
> If something **goes** with something else, ...

The pronoun *something* can be qualified:

> If something such as success, glory or love **evades** you, ...
> If something such as an idea or subject **fits** something, ...
> If something, for example paint, **flakes**, ...
> If something unpleasant **sets in** , ...

If there is an accent on the plural, *things* can replace *something*:

> If things such as ideas, beliefs or statements **sweep** a place ...

Where the likely subject is extremely restricted, it can be named:

> If a play is **taken off**, ...
> When an object **breaks**, ...
> When the sun **sets**, ...

This structure allows the use of a fairly general subject as well as specific ones:

> If a powerful force **tears** something from somewhere, ...
> When jelly, glue, cement, or some other soft or liquid substance **sets**.

Mixed subjects

Quite commonly a verb has a sense where the subject can be either animate or inanimate. No suitable pronoun exists in English for this usage, so we have to resort to clumsier expressions:

> If someone or something **degenerates**, ...
> If someone or something **falls**, ...
> If someone or something **captivates** you, ...

With plural forms, this becomes:

> When things or people **disappoint** you, ...

Operators

In the examples given so far, it will have been noticed that they all start with an operator, either *if* or *when*. The Cobuild dictionary compilers

OPERATOR	CO-TEXT (1)					TOPIC	CO-TEXT (2)	
CONJUNCTION	SUBJECT					PREDICATOR	OBJECT	ADJUNCT
	MODIFIER	HEAD	BRANCHES	QUALIFIER	EXEMPLIFICATION			
		you					someone	
		people						PREP PHRASE
	a (adjective) the	NOUN	(or NOUN/ LIST)	(who is etc.) (PREP PHRASE)	(especially NOUN/LIST)	VERB	(you) (NOUN PHRASE)	(PREP PHRASE)
if when		someone	(or something)		(such as NOUN PHRASE/LIST)			
		something			(for example NOUN PHRASE/ LIST)			

Table 3: Structural options in the first part of Cobuild verb explanations

chose whichever was the more comfortable expression. The result seems to be that in relation to people and animals, *if* introduces an activity which is broadly speaking within the discretion of the individual, whereas there is rather more inevitability about *when*. With *when,* the relation between subject and verb is a little more mutually determined. So, since sewing and skiing are typically human activities, they are introduced by *when*. But rioting and burgling, while still recognizably human, are not typical, and so are introduced by *if*.

In relation to inanimate objects, a similar distinction is observed. If the action seems to be inherent in the nature of the object, for example, *to break* the operator will be *when*; *when* also with *the sun sets*. If the action is only something that might happen, then *if* is used.

Summary

The structural options that have been identified so far do not present a very formidable array, and the main lines can be set out simply as in Table 3. This shows how the first parts of the verb explanations are tackled. Verb explanations are the most structurally complex, and the other parts of speech will show fewer options. Idiomatic phrases require some special attention.

Analysis of the second part

The analysis of the second part of the explanations of words proceeds along similar lines. There are references back to elements of the first part, and then a string structure of chunks adding explanatory detail.

First chunk

The first chunk of the second part of the statements is now further described, returning to the original examples of several different parts of speech, as in Table 1. In many examples, some of the words recall words in the co-text, either by repetition or other types of cohesion. These are called the *framework* of the explanation. The remainder of the first chunk is a rephrasing of the topic, and is called the *gloss*. So in the examples given, the analysis is as follows in Table 4:

First Part	Second Part			
	OPERATOR		GLOSS	
A house	is	a	building	
If you **defeat** someone		you	win a victory over	them
A **pure** substance	is		not mixed with anything else	
If something happens **often**		it happens	many times	

Table 4: Analysis of the second part

Of the items in the framework, *a, you,* and *happens* are repetitions of words in the co-text, and *it* and *them* are pronouns which refer back as follows:

it refers back to *something;*
them refers back to *someone.*

This analysis permits us to isolate the gloss element and study its role and function. In the examples above:

a. *building* is a replacement of *house*, and we can assume that the two words are in a recognizable semantic relation - in this case hyponomy, with *building* the superordinate. The following chunk *in which people live* provides a restriction on building, giving a classic definition:

superordinate restriction

This can be paraphrased as 'a house is a type of building. It is different from other types of building by the fact that people live in it.'

b. *win a victory over* replaces *defeat. Defeat* is a transitive verb, with the object *someone* in the co-text. In the comment, the verb is replaced by a structure with a verb, its object, and a preposition. The object of the original verb now becomes the object of the preposition.

c. *not mixed with anything else* replaces *pure*. Here the explanation hinges on the negative, and the semantic relation is antonymy. The adjective is replaced by a past participle and an adjunct.

133

d. *many times* replaces *often*, the adverb giving way to a nominal group.

Second chunk

The second chunks of Table 1 relate to the first chunks in ways which have already been met in the first part analysis (see Table 5).

Second part, second chunk	Analysis
in which people live	qualifier of headword building
in a contest	adjunct
such as a battle, game or argument	exemplification list of nouns
or much of the time	branch

Table 5: Analysis of second chunks

Discussion

The outline analysis of the language of lexical statement shows a slight specialization of the normal conventions of English. The only physical difference is the identification of the topic by using bold face, and the analysis hinges on this. The rules of English grammar and semantics are unaffected.

The Cobuild dictionary compilers, who made an explanatory style out of a set of guide-lines, worked without restraint and used their natural choices of language to express the meanings that they wanted to convey. Several stages of consultative editing reduced the range of different structures to what is published, and work since then has made further rationalizations.

There is no particular communicative virtue in having an obviously formulaic style of explanation. Traditional dictionaries use a set of compression techniques which require specific decoding skills, and in rejecting these in favour of ordinary English it would be counterproductive to return to a formula in disguise. Rigid rules of compilation lull compilers into a false sense of security, and may obscure important distinctions of usage. For some applications, the repetitive simplicity of formulae may give greater accessibility than more accurate and varied expressions. Equally, there is some point in cutting down variation that seems over-subtle for the kind of communication in which it appears.

A dictionary is a text in which most units of discourse are very brief, and in which the overall structure is highly repetitive. The user will naturally be led to expect that the same kind of type-face, or the same kind of phraseology, will carry the same sort of information. The reverse of this is that differences are meaningful, and so phraseology should be standardized at least to the point where differences can be justified.

Applications

There are a number of applications of the kind of analysis presented here. First of all, it will be possible to make an exhaustive comparison of actual dictionary writing. The analysis will be a professional tool with which the wording of dictionaries can be improved. Lexicographers will be able to consider alternative expressions, knowing exactly how they differ. Problem areas, for example adjectives, can be experimented with in a systematic way. The vocabulary and syntax of lexical statement will be made explicit, so that people can understand how and why meanings are explained.

Secondly, the description will be a part of the general description of English. Since the Cobuild type of explanation relies on the natural use of words, there are no new conventions to learn. The structures and meanings set out in this chapter have been derived from the dictionary text, not prescribed in advance.

The same cannot be said for most dictionary definitions, which are very obscurely structured for anyone approaching from normal English. Because of some long-established habits (for example, that the first part must be the topic only) and a great concern for compression, they require rules as if they were written in another language. So the structural resources of English are hardly available to the compilers in this kind of lexicography, and the explanations of this type of conventional dictionary are not able to be assimilated into the general repertoire of the user.

Inferences and implications

The analysis has shown that each explanation gives rise to a number of entailments, implications, and inferences. For example, the first verb explanation is phrased as follows:

> If you defeat someone, you win a victory over them in a contest such as a battle, game or argument.

Immediately, we can assume that, in these circumstances (and not necessarily always),

a battle is a contest
a game is a contest
an argument is a contest
you defeat someone in a contest
defeating someone means winning a victory over them
you win a victory over someone in a contest

The subject of *defeat* is *you*, so we can infer that defeating is not considered an unusual or reprehensible activity. The operator is *if*, signifying that it is not an inherent activity, but one that the human race is distinctly likely to indulge in from time to time. The object of *defeat* is *someone*, indicating that defeating is done to a person, but not a specially selected one.

So the combination of the general conventions of English and the particular conventions of the Cobuild dictionary are powerful in interpreting the explanations.

Conclusion

The language we use to explain the meaning of words is an important part of our linguistic repertoire. In the style studied here, it is clearly only a slight extension of the ordinary use of English. Thus, all the flexibility of a natural language is available for implications, inferences, etc. In turn, these can be developed into a set of tools by which dictionaries can be constructed and understood. All sorts of valuable semantic and structural statements can be retrieved.

For the future, this analysis offers the possibility of harnessing one of the most powerful, but least understood, features of a natural language—the features of paraphrase. The lexical statements set up equivalences, which are found in the topic and gloss categories. See Table 6 for an analysis of our original examples:

Topic (Table 1)		Gloss (Table 4)
house	=	building
defeat	=	win a victory over
pure	=	not mixed with anything else
often	=	many times

Table 6: Paraphrase

The analysis will establish that *building* is a superordinate of *house*, and the rest are synonymic. The grammatical replacement shown, for example, in *defeat - win a victory over* will also be made explicit. This activity, if carried out thoroughly and accurately, is a reasonable model for the understanding of the text.

That is to say, if a person can routinely rephrase a given sentence in his or her own words and state the difference between the two sentences in a third sentence, that person will be seen as understanding the language. If a machine can perform in a similar way, the machine can reasonably be described as understanding the language. And once a machine can be seen as understanding a language, the map of information technology will have to be re-drawn.

Summing up

This book is an attempt to show that there is a lot more to learn about the English language than it was possible to imagine a few years ago. It has been suspected, of course, in all the work on idiom usage that has accumulated in language teaching materials. While grammars and dictionaries continue to report the structure of language as if it could be neatly divided, many of those people who are professionally engaged in handling language have known in their bones that the division into grammar and vocabulary obscures a very central area of meaningful organization. In fact, it may well be argued on the basis of the work in this book that when we have thoroughly pursued the patterns of co-occurrence of linguistic choices there will be little or no need for a separate residual grammar or lexicon.

That remains to be seen. Certainly, the first application of computers to the study of language corpora has uncovered a lot of new facts which have to be built in to our descriptions of languages. And it should be stressed that this book reports only the first dipping of an inquisitive toe into the vast pool of language texts. The corpus of the 1980s, although boasting a central size of 20 million words, will be seen in another decade as a relatively modest repository of evidence; the software tools increase in sophistication month by month, and must still be regarded as primitive compared with what the real needs are. Most limiting of all, our concepts, our ideas of what to expect and how to understand what we are observing, are not keeping pace with the evidence available. There is as yet little or no discussion at an international level and, beyond the Cobuild project, no thorough exploitation of corpus linguistics.

Appendix I

Sample text

There are many kinds of activity, and communication is only one of them, although often it does not look much like activity. The shelves of a library can look very inactive indeed, and someone sitting with his eyes shut listening to a transistor through earphones may seem fairly static. But in a library we see a stage of communication where the activity is halted in time. If we consider the whole process, the activity is obvious enough. The nervous activity of authors is legendary, and the silent reader in his armchair is making continuous, fast, and precise eye movements. And, like the radio listener, his brain is highly active if he is taking anything in.

There are many kinds of communication, too, and human communication through language is only a small sub-section, although it is very important. Attempts to set out the special characteristics of human language have become quite sophisticated. But research workers have now created most aspects of human verbal communication in animals and machines. Perhaps mankind's only remaining boast is that we thought of it first! It is certainly an intricate and distinctive kind of activity.

Figure 1: the first order word list

there	2	through	2	he	1
are	2	earphones	1	taking	1
many	2	may	1	anything	1
kinds	2	seem	1	too	1
of	10	fairly	1	human	3
activity	6	static	1	language	2
and	8	but	2	small	1
communication	5	in	5	sub-section	1
is	11	we	3	important	1
only	3	see	1	attempts	1
one	1	stage	1	set	1
them	1	where	1	out	1
although	2	halted	1	special	1
often	1	time	1	characteristics	1
it	4	if	2	have	1
does	1	consider	1	become	1
not	1	whole	1	quite	1
look	2	process	1	sophisticated	1
much	1	obvious	1	research	1
like	2	enough	1	workers	1
the	8	nervous	1	now	1
shelves	1	authors	1	recreated	1
a	5	legendary	1	most	1
library	2	silent	1	aspects	1
can	1	reader	1	verbal	1
very	2	armchair	1	animals	1
inactive	1	making	1	machines	1
indeed	1	continuous	1	perhaps	1
someone	1	fast	1	mankind's	1
sitting	1	precise	1	remaining	1
with	1	eye	1	boast	1
his	3	movements	1	that	1
eyes	1	radio	1	thought	1
shut	1	listener	1	first	1
listening	1	brain	1	certainly	1
to	2	highly	1	an	1
transistor	1	active	1	intricate	1
				distinctive	1
				kind	1

Figure 2: alphabetical order word list

5	a	2	if	1	radio
1	active	1	important	1	reader
6	activity	5	in	1	recreated
2	although	1	inactive	1	remaining
1	an	1	indeed	1	research
8	and	1	intricate	1	see
1	animals	11	is	1	seem
1	anything	4	it	1	set
2	are	1	kind	1	shelves
1	armchair	2	kinds	1	shut
1	aspects	2	language	1	silent
1	attempts	1	legendary	1	sitting
1	authors	2	library	1	small
1	become	2	like	1	someone
1	boast	1	listener	1	sophisticated
1	brain	1	listening	1	special
2	but	2	look	1	stage
1	can	1	machines	1	static
1	certainly	1	making	1	sub-section
1	characteristics	1	mankind's	1	taking
5	communication	2	many	1	that
1	consider	1	may	8	the
1	continuous	1	most	1	them
1	distinctive	1	movements	2	there
1	does	1	much	1	thought
1	earphones	1	nervous	2	through
1	enough	1	not	1	time
1	eye	1	now	2	to
1	eyes	1	obvious	1	too
1	fairly	10	of	1	transistor
1	fast	1	often	1	verbal
1	first	1	one	2	very
1	halted	3	only	3	we
1	have	1	out	1	where
1	he	1	perhaps	1	whole
1	highly	1	precise	1	with
3	his	1	process	1	workers
3	human	1	quite		

Figure 3: frequency order word list

11	is	1	brain	1	one
10	of	1	can	1	out
8	and	1	certainly	1	perhaps
8	the	1	characteristics	1	precise
6	activity	1	consider	1	process
5	a	1	continuous	1	quite
5	communication	1	distinctive	1	radio
5	in	1	does	1	reader
4	it	1	earphones	1	recreated
3	his	1	enough	1	remaining
3	human	1	eye	1	research
3	only	1	eyes	1	see
3	we	1	fairly	1	seem
2	although	1	fast	1	set
2	are	1	first	1	shelves
2	but	1	halted	1	shut
2	have	1	he	1	silent
2	if	1	highly	1	sitting
2	kinds	1	important	1	small
2	language	1	inactive	1	someone
2	library	1	indeed	1	sophisticated
2	like	1	intricate	1	special
2	look	1	kind	1	stage
2	many	1	legendary	1	static
2	there	1	listener	1	sub-section
2	through	1	listening	1	taking
2	to	1	machines	1	that
2	very	1	making	1	them
1	active	1	mankind's	1	thought
1	an	1	may	1	time
1	animals	1	most	1	too
1	anything	1	movements	1	transistor
1	armchair	1	much	1	verbal
1	aspects	1	nervous	1	where
1	attempts	1	not	1	whole
1	authors	1	now	1	with
1	become	1	obvious	1	workers
1	boast	1	often		

Figure 4: Cobuild frequency count—the top 113 forms

the	309497	were	18547	only	8889
of	155044	which	18344	it's	8848
and	153801	an	17446	will	8834
to	137056	so	17433	than	8315
a	129928	what	16434	yes	8234
in	100138	their	16160	just	8190
that	67042	if	16008	because	8128
I	64849	would	14687	two	7334
it	61379	about	14547	over	7285
was	54722	no	14386	don't	7253
is	49186	said	14163	get	7241
he	42057	up	13552	see	7216
for	40857	when	13501	any	7029
you	37477	been	13417	much	6795
on	35951	out	13361	way	6791
with	35844	them	13322	these	6791
as	34755	do	12943	how	6758
'	30952	my	12761	down	6755
be	29799	more	12718	even	6609
had	29592	who	12708	first	6410
but	29572	me	11697	did	6220
they	29512	like	11564	back	6201
at	28958	very	11483	got	6190
his	26491	can	11271	our	6189
have	26113	has	11241	new	6127
not	25419	him	11110	go	6029
this	25185	some	10537	most	5893
are	23372	into	10414	where	5920
or	22445	then	10265	after	5797
by	21916	now	10246	your	5740
we	20964	think	10007	say	5636
she	20958	well	9654	man	5339
from	20933	know	9549	er	5277
one	20354	time	9481	little	5260
all	20022	could	9214	too	5210
–	19736	people	9083	many	5182
there	19145	its	9061	good	5180
her	18916	other	8904		

Figure 5: word frequency profile (1)

Word-form count	Number such	Vocabulary total	% of vocabulary	Word-form total	% of text
1	85	85	75.22	85	44.97
2	15	100	88.50	115	60.85
3	4	104	92.04	127	67.20
4	1	105	92.92	131	69.31
5	3	108	95.58	146	77.25
6	1	109	96.46	152	80.42
8	2	111	98.23	168	88.89
10	1	112	99.12	178	94.18
11	1	113	100.00	189	100.00

Figure 6: word frequency profile (2)

Word-form count	Number such	Vocabulary total	% of vocabulary	Word-form total	% of text
11	1	1	0.88	11	5.82
10	1	2	1.77	21	11.11
8	2	4	3.54	37	19.58
6	1	5	4.42	43	22.75
5	3	8	7.08	58	30.69
4	1	9	7.96	62	32.80
3	4	13	11.50	74	39.15
2	15	28	24.78	104	55.03
1	85	113	100.00	189	100.00

Figure 7

Blood	AE12	1050	Blood	AU	415	Bloom	SAA	1120
	AE12	1209		AU	608		T27	10
	AE12	1216		AU	609		NS	1
	AE12	1254		WB	91		G4	211
	AE12	1309		WB	382		AE10	450
	AE12	1376		WB	402		AE11	41
	OAL	271		WB	439		KT3	83

	OAL	404		M15	101		HIF	47
	AF	79		M15	114		HIF	169
	DO	29		M15	120		WB	532
	DO	68		M15	202		AS	51
	DO	136		M15	631	Bloomed	M12	526
	KT1	19		M15	685	Blooming	HP	40
	KT1	145		M15	710		SAA	562
	KT1	468		GP	111		T23	61
	KT2	96		CI	41		AK	149
	KT2	127		CI	603		J3	191
	KT2	189		ETP	29		SLT2	13
	KT2	199		STP	24		MC	31
	KT2	317		AS	40		G2	99
Bloodier	KT2	329		ET	9		AE3	440
Bloodily	KT2	572		ESH	1		AE4	43
Bloodless	KT2	583		HAP	1565		AE5	386
	KT3	138		AE2	739		AE5	449
	KT3	346		AE11	651		AE7	78
	KT3	499		M11	480		AE7	658
Bloodshot	KT3	527		M15	285		AE12	37
Bloody	KT3	604		AM	220		AE12	578
	KT3	629		EM	17		OAL	64
	KT3	706		SCD2	3		OAE1	24
	KT3	753		SCD2	24		AF	10
	KT3	824		PAR	7		MG	15
	KT3	989		DA	122		B	51
	TJD	89		AA	1014		CAM	159
	TJD	110		SAA	770		AS	59
	TJD	159		EDGA	16		G1	273
	M8	22		PD	59		G4	269
	M8	39		HAP	35		FL	14
	M8	119		HAP	1368		FL	105
	M8	154		HAP	1675	Bloomy	BR	13
	M8	178		HAP	1952		AE9	276
	M8	195		HAP	1986		FL	343
	M8	209		HAP	2365	Blossom	PC1	4
	M8	241		J3	67		BR	16
	M8	286		J3	399	Blossomed	ETG	7
	M8	298		J6	857	Blossoms	SMA	30
	M8	309		J10	268		HAP	1847

(Montgomery, 1967)

Figure 8: concordance to is: *eleven occurrences*

of activity and communication	is	only one of them
communication where the activity	is	halted in time if
whole process the activity	is	obvious enough the nervous
nervous activity of authors	is	legendary and the silent
reader in his armchair	is	making continuous fast and
radio listener his brain	is	highly active if he
highly active if he	is	taking anything in there
human communication through language	is	only a small sub-section
small sub-section although it	is	very important attempts to
mankind's only remaining boast	is	that we thought of
of it first it	is	certainly an intricate and

Figure 9: concordance to is: *sentences*

There are many kinds of activity, and
communication   is   only one of them, although
often it does not look much
like activity.

But in a library we see a stage of
communication where the activity   is   halted in time.

If we consider the whole process, the
activity   is   obvious enough.

The nervous activity of authors   is   legendary, and the silent
reader in his armchair is
making continuous, fast,
and precise eye movements.

The nervous activity of authors is
legendary, and the silent reader in
his armchair   is   making continuous, fast,
and precise eye movements.

And, like the radio listener, his brain   is   highly active if he is taking anything in.

And, like the radio listener, his brain is highly active if he   is   taking anything in.

There are many kinds of communication, too, and human communication through language   is   only a small sub-section, although it is very important.

There are many kinds of communication, too, and human communication through language is only a small sub-section, although it   is   very important.

Perhaps mankind's only remaining boast   is   that we thought of it first!

It   is   certainly an intricate and distinctive kind of activity.

Figure 10

of it first it	is	certainly an intricate and
communication where the activity	is	halted in time if
radio listener his brain	is	highly active if he
nervous activity of authors	is	legendary and the silent
reader in his armchair	is	making continuous fast and
whole process the activity	is	obvious enough the nervous
human communication through language	is	only a small sub-section
of activity and communication	is	only one of them
highly active if he	is	taking anything in there
mankind's only remaining boast	is	that we thought of
small sub-sections although it	is	very important attempts to

Figure 11

human communication through language	is	only a small sub-section
highly active if he	is	taking anything in there
radio listener his brain	is	highly active if he
of activity and communication	is	only one of them
reader in his armchair	is	making continuous fast and
nervous activity of authors	is	legendary and the silent
small sub-section although it	is	very important attempts to
of it first it	is	certainly an intricate and
mankind's only remaining boast	is	that we thought of
communication where the activity	is	halted in time if
whole process the activity	is	obvious enough the nervous

Figure 12: concordance to is: ± *4 words: alphabetical list*

a	1	highly	2	radio	1
active	2	his	2	reader	1
activity	4	human	1	remaining	1
although	1	if	3	silent	1
an	1	important	1	small	2
and	4	in	3	sub-section	2
anything	1	intricate	1	taking	1
armchair	1	it	3	that	1
attempts	1	language	1	the	4
authors	1	legendary	1	them	1
boast	1	listener	1	there	1
brain	1	mankind's	1	thought	1
certainly	1	making	1	through	1
communication	3	nervous	2	time	1
continuous	1	obvious	1	to	1
enough	1	of	5	very	1
fast	1	one	1	we	1
first	1	only	3	where	1
halted	1	process	1	whole	1
he	2				

Figure 13: concordance to is: ± *4: frequency list*

of	5	a	1	mankind's	1
		although	1	making	1
activity	4	an	1	obvious	1
and	4	anything	1	out	1
the	4	armchair	1	process	1
		attempts	1	radio	1
communication	3	authors	1	reader	1
if	3	boast	1	remaining	1
in	3	brain	1	silent	1
it	3	certainly	1	taking	1
only	3	continuous	1	that	1
		enough	1	them	1
active	2	fast	1	there	1
he	2	first	1	thought	1
highly	2	halted	1	through	1
his	2	human	1	time	1
nervous	2	important	1	to	1
small	2	intricate	1	very	1
sub-section	2	language	1	we	1
		legendary	1	where	1
		listener	1	whole	1

Figure 14: text analysis statistics

Length of the text in word-forms	189	
No. of different word-forms	113	
Length of the text in characters	940	
Average word length	4.97	
Longest word	15	
Length of the text in sentences	11	
Average sentence length in word-forms	17.18	
The longest sentence	28	
No. of sentences with less than 10 word-forms	0	0.00%
No. of sentences with 11 to 20 word-forms	7	63.64%
No. of sentences with 21 to 30 word-forms	4	36.36%
No. of sentences with 31 to 40 word-forms	0	0.00%
No. of sentences with more than 41 word-forms	0	0.00%

Appendix II

SECTION A *Declined* in Sense 1

1. d the Governor in respect to Hearst.' When Hearst
2. ndidate for East Surrey. But on each occasion, he
3. ng <P 208> was to say: "Have some eland", which I
4. MSELF STRONGLY IN FAVOUR OF FREE SPEECH. BUT HE
5. ived at the television studio perfectly sober and
6. ket of Bastos, offered one to the Englishman, who
7. article on "Male chauvinism, British style." She
8. ounced before telling him about it, he gracefully
9. ipal Ownership League on 4 October 1905, modestly
10. ph was in his own performance. The battles he had
11. g it all at Sujhir's disposal. <P 214> but Sudhir
12. n we asked Gopal if he would not dance for us, he
13. last Friday "the darkest [night] of my life"—and
14. chool in the pony trap for the Easter Egg Hunt. I
15. us: he had asked an enormous fee, we regretfully
16. ython era was invited to appear in this film but
17. tled down his throat. He offered me the bottle. I
18. ady wished to see me urgently. I made excuses and
19. trip on this railway from Greenwich to London. He
20. t a special part was being written in for him. He
21. an think of no way of stopping him, though he has
22. ement and to avoid the fellow-traveller's tag. He
23. ng them. (He was very impatient with students who
24. nd grew their hair but a few of the more ruthless
25. ned the invasion in the most forthright terms but
26. e allowed to address the Court, but the Governors
27. at at short notice." The Vice-Chancellor's Office
28. ake it worse!' [w?—Ed.]e frequently had requests, always
29. the cause of death was not made public, Mr Santos
30. ; except one, ex-President Grover Cleveland, who
31. ave other qualities," said Oliver Barrett III but
32. was now to enter—the lad gravely and resolutely
33. ion. I think it very significant that the UDA had
34. isitor. What if I had turned the handle, the door
35. that the four-man crew included one Briton, but
36. himself strongly in favour of free speech. But he

declined,   Al   Smith   continued   with   his   meeting,   den

declined.   He   was   a   zeaous   Cobdenite   freetrader   wh

declined.   It   was   a   dish   of   minced   eland,   the   big   b

DECLINED   TO   RE-PUDIATE   CONTROVERSIAL   TACTICS   OF

declined   all   refreshments   thereafter,   but   absurd,

declined,   and   lit   one   for   himself.   "That   is   not   so

declined,   and   they   didn't   ask   again.   She   found   she

declined   and   shortly   afterwards   Sir   Robert   Bignold

declined,   and   then   accepted   five   days   later   as   a   p

declined   else-where,   he   won   in   the   face   below   his

declined   everything,   even   to   sit   down,   so   they   par

declined   firmly   but   said   his   Gura   would   perform   in

declined   further   comment.   The   last   word   belonged   t

declined   her   offer.   She   urged   that   I   should   suppor

declined   his   services.   There   was   an   awkward   interv

declined   it—because   I   think   Brooks   has   actually

declined   it,   as   he   knew   I   would.   I   had   rather   kiss

declined   politely   but   two   minutes   later   my   bedroom

declined   saying   it   was   a   "needless   risk   to   run".   A

declined   the   offer   and   returned   to   his   garret.   I

declined   the   invitation   to   address   Boon   as   "Charle

declined   to   speak   at   the   Labour   Party   rally   in   Hyd

declined   to   copy.)   He   had   trouble   with   upright   sha

declined   to   do   so,   they   had   clearly   not   addressed

declined   to   take   any   action   whatever,   however   dipl

declined   to   give   an   immediate   answer   to   the   studen

declined   to   comment.—Rummidge   Morning   Post   RIOT

declined,   to   keep   things   out   of   the   paper.   Several

declined   to   comment.   Brody   looked   up   from   the   pap

declined   to   allow   his   sorrow   for   those   who   died   to

declined   to   elaborate.   (I   doubt   if   he   could   have.)

declined   to   carry   the   thing   a   step   further.   And   at

declined   to   attend   this   mass   rally   in   the   past,   a

declined   to   open   and   someone   had   observed   my   actio

declined   to   identify   him.   The   others   were   said   by

declined   to   repudiate   controversial   tactics   of   peo

SECTION B *Declined*—remainder of concordance

1. its contribution to national student politics has
2. ts, did they not, Clay Jones? Jones: They rapidly
3. spiral could get worse, as the level of activity
4. ntries—real <P 67> disposable spending power has
5. licy towards the west, her active involvement has
6. know that the sort of lot of people generally has
7. In 1966. But since 1971 the WPPE's influence has
8. ian Defence, the Muzio Gambit, the Queen's Gambit
9. nt, and in that one Month, the crime rate sharply
10. attlefield, as distinct from the rear areas, soon
11. izon became level and blue and clipped as the sun
12. t that our industrial performance has relatively
13. made her an importer. The value of her currency
14. he had not read the report. Slowly, the industry
15. 5, pressure in the United States since prices have
16. he Second World War, modernist Fine Art in France
17. es also miners or railway workers, for so long in
18. , psychology and so on, and they've certainly not
19. workers in the total working population actually
20. p's own interest in the physical side of marriage
21. from 18 to 9 percent of the market; Lucky Strike
22. d so far, and had been told so often that she had
23. number of paddy holdings, and their average size
24. he share of the rural areas in total population
25. in terms of seats: the number of Congress Members
26. ain's share of the world shipbuilding had as a result
27. rship has stagnated and its electoral performance
28. in March (and a revision discovered they had not
29. farms and farm families in New England has not
30. instead. Surprisingly, however, this tendency has
31. per head of population has in some cases actually
32. oded messages received by the ordinary person has
33. t, let alone against a Labour government. The RCP
34. —s this still the case, or have social sciences
35. t the British Aircraft Industry is defunct; it's
36. ited range fires. But the number of prairie fires
37. ehaves in imagination. It may be that Britain had
38. nization. With many thousands in jail, membership
39. , it is true that the authority of parliament has
40. rate. "The average age of dwellings has steadily

declined.
declined,
declined,
declined.
declined.
declined.
declined.
declined.
declined.
declined.
declined.
declined.
declined
declined,
declined,
declined
declined
declined
declined
declined
declined,
declined
declined
declined
declined
declined
declined
declined
declined
declined
declined
declined
declined
declined
declined
declined
declined
declined
declined
declined
declined,
declined,

Attempts to launch an Alternative left o
Bill Sowerbutts. Often, they would disa
But, on Keynesian arguments, this could
But for how long will the trade unions a
But in the visits of British Maoists to
((C)) Oh, it has. There are figures to p
Frequent changes of address, the failure
Most of them are not only learned for t
Our Political Opponents and other Bodies
Refugees were posing an acute and growin
That was another time of comparative coo
against that of other countries. If
along with the purchasing power of her
and its members took up other activities
and costs have gone up," explained a GE
and fell; in Britain it barely survived
and troubled industries. Many varied moti
as a whole. Our numbers of applications e
between 1911 and 1941'. Class divisions w
but he persuaded himself that this was o
even more sharply, from 14 to 6 per cent.
even further, that she eagerly adopted th
from four-fifths to half an acre. Many
from an average of 84 percent in 1950 to
from 371 to 361; the CPI stayed steady at
from 50% in 1914 to under 10% in 1964. In
further, a whole range of new organisatio
in February after all). Wage settlement
in 1970, and the average age of farmers
in the mid-1970s, and savings have remain
in the last ten years among the developin
in favour of coded messages. We may guess
in spirit and in numbers and in 1949 diss
in undergraduate popularity? Well, first
of course: the Americans are the leaders
sharply with the white man's arrival. As
so far, and had been told so often that s
to half a million by late 1936, and the a
with the growth of the great producer in
writes E. F. Carter of the Stanford Res

Appendix III

Table 1: co-ordination of sense and syntax: summary

Sense	Syntax	Total	Yield	Yielded	Yielding	Yields
give way	intr. verb	33	16	9	5	3
produce	noun headword	30	10			20
leads to	trans. verb	18	6	6	3	3
		81				
Minor usages						
surrender	trans. verb	10	4	3	3	3
produce	trans. verb	7	3	3	1	1
	noun modifier	1			1	
		18				
Minor senses						
collapse	intr. verb	4	3	1		
	noun modifier	5	5			
	noun headword	4			4	
		13				
soft	participle modifier	2			2	
merge	intr. verb	1				1
unclassified	participle cluster	1			1	
		4				
Phrases						
surrender	*yield up* (trans. verb)	6	3	3		
produce	trans. verb (Obj. *profit*)	3	1			2
		9				
Totals		125	51	25	20	29

Table 2: co-ordination of sense and syntax

Sense	Syntax	Yield	Yielded	Yielding	Yields
give way	intr. verb	14	52	84	103
		19	53	89	122
		24	56	93	123
		34	62	94	
		35	67	96	
		36	68		
		37	69		
		38	70		
		39	71		
		40			
		41			
		42			
		43			
		44			
		45			
		46			
produce	noun headword	1			97
		10			98
		17			99
		20			100
		21			104
		25			106
		26			107
		27			108
		32			109
		51			110
					111
					112
					113
					114
					117
					118
					120
					124
					125
leads to	trans. verb	11	54	83	115
		13	55	85	119
		15	60	88	121
		18	61		
		23	59		
		30	64		*(cont.)*

Table 2: co-ordination of sense and syntax (cont.)

Sense	Syntax	Yield	Yielded	Yielding	Yields
		Minor usages			
surrender, abandon	trans. verb	16	63	77	
		22	65	90	
		31	66	95	
		33			
produce	trans. verb	9	57	86	
		12	58		
		28	76		
	noun modifier			91	
		Minor senses			
collapse	intr. verb	2	72		
		3			
		47			
	noun modifier	4			
		5			
		6			
		7			
		8			
	noun headword			78	
				79	
				81	
				82	
soft				80	
				87	
merge					116
unclassified				92	
		Phrases			
surrender, abandon	*yield up* trans. verb	48	73		
		49	74		
		50	75		
produce	trans. verb obj. *profit*	29			101
					102

Concordance to the lemma yield

yield
1. that could fire a nuclear shell with a 15 kiloton
   yield about the same size bomb which destroyed
2. O: Hm Hm T1: You see if it does. Then we it will
   yield just the same way as a tensile specimen. I
3. You reach the yield stress and then it starts to
   yield plastically (4) and then it comes out as S1.
4. Re (4) and. You will get yielding then when the
   yield stress the average yield stress v divided b
5. T yielding then when the yield stress the average
   yield stress v divided by the area. Which is a (
6. uh t: and that will collapse essentially when the
   yield stress the average stress across here is eq
7. ng. And then to see whether that does reach the
   yield stress for plastic deformation or not S10:
8. pecimen. Is being stretched until you reach the
   yield stress and then it starts to yield plastical
9. atures against it. The traditional human IQ tests
   yield a score which runs between 0 and an upper li
10. f Saving Certificates, but with the new one, the
    yield after only 12 months is 9% and the average r
11. the interaction of these different approaches to
    yield an effective answer ((Chapter six)) The thi
12. llon of water. Only two domestic baths full would
    yield an incredible solid pound of bacteria. The
13. electrical significance but which did not seem to
    yield any satisfactory bell ringing inside, or
14. but Davis. Was Cynthia, he wondered, beginning to
    yield at last to the long siege? Was that why she
15. s painted in front, where the dry dust refused to
    yield even a weed. Above the picture, stamped in
16. e Soviet Union, remains adamant that it will not
    yield even a limited measure of editorial control
17. ng problem in overpopulated lands: increasing the
    yield for a given area. They cannot be grown close
18. movements. On the crest of the passes, the rocks
    yield fossils. They are not very many, but if yo
19. st powerful government in western Europe had to
    yield in a conflict with the weakest and most divi
20. ns, or about 50,000 tons of TNT, while the H-bomb
    yield is almost unlimited. The Soviet Union, for

21.   does. The more labour you devote to it, the more
      yield it will produce, and the ultimate limits of

22.   Any society that hopes to be stable must surely
      yield its most passionate prejudices in the cause

23.   ong the reason why it has not worked may actually
      yield more information than if it had worked.

24.   ategy. But we did not yield then and we shall not
      yield now.' On the wall of his office, Professor

25.   typical backward country, Nyasaland, the expected
      yield of graduates from internal sources— from

26.   ve power is referred to as the 'yield'. Thus, the
      yield of the two bombs dropped on Hiroshima and Na

27.   nuclear tests and prohibited tests which exceed a
      yield of 150 kilotons—the equivalent of 1590,000

28.   marginal peasant's holding of 0.23 acres would
      yield only 200 pounds of rice or less. Annual de

29.   agreed prices which they knew were very likely to
      yield profits that the Ministry would not regard

30.   t'. Expressing feelings and "talking through" may
      yield satisfactions to the Parent and the Child

31.   e to one, but they were obliged in the process to
      yield some fifteen to twenty kilometres. With

32.   it the water 100 per cent and have a far better
      yield than any farm round here for miles. Our

33.   itary victory over the Cuban rebels, unwilling to
      yield the concessions that would defuse the disput

34.   tory, was Hitler's basic strategy. But we did not
      yield then and we shall not yield now'. On the

35.   Watergate conversation, which Mr. Nixon agreed to
      yield to the courts, 'did not exist'. As it happe

36.   f you have serious stain problems that just won't
      yield to elbow grease, these tips from Ideal Stand

37.   ee months or so. Eventually, they are forced to
      yield to stronger, more rested rivals and they

38.   wilderness of gaunt and spooky warehousing is to
      yield to complete redevelopment. Elsewhere Covent

39.   rom Bond Street and Mayfair. Though Turkish baths
      yield to saunas, here, at Floris, he can buy hair

40.   a shawl to intone: 'Ndiyavuma.! Nidiyavuma!' ('I
      yield to the spirits!'). I checked in at the Gord

41.   as his oyster and its inhabitants his servants to
      yield to his whims. George was engrossed in minin

42. modernise their precepts of Judaic orthodoxy, and
    yield to the demands of Western culture as well as
43. rough the air and as something in him refused to
    yield to unconsciousness, he came by degrees to id
44. you. It's because I've long ago decided always to
    yield to my cowardice. I was afraid of Philip the
45. y of them. But it's become a principle with me to
    yield to my fear of people. I propitiate them, or
46. bject that radio has long been under pressure to
    yield to television, but the poet and critic Pete
47. es to a filing cabinet. The latter, however, will
    yield to a jemmy and a bit of brute force, while t
48. psychiatry (including methods of making the brain
    yield up its secrets) to begin to be able to put t
49. rewell ... Our forfeited garden of Eden, Joyous I
    yield up for thee my sad life And were it far br
50. y the 1980s, large areas of medical practice will
    yield up their secrets to the computer. The first
51. -crunching, they begin to have far more dramatic
    yield when the power of the computer is directed

yielded

52. iving on to the Park, even the clubs have all but
    yielded. I will start just a little way up (east
53. I'd appreciate it.' Feynon pulled in breath, and
    yielded. 'I'll see what I can do.' He tucked his
54. ions between Chestnut and Beardsley, one of which
    yielded a shadow of the fiend (N. Petit, Larousse
55. nce a hole in the wall behind Whistler's 'Mother'
    yielded as much as twenty-four dollars and some ch
56. to Denmark and Sweden. In Sweden the authorities
    yielded at once to the threats which swiftly follo
57. re than recoup these costs from the extra harvest
    yielded: but in the meantime he needs credit to t
58. ongress will spend every penny — and more — that is
    yielded by taxes. A cut in taxes will mean a cut
59. Fascinating glimpses of collaboration have been
    yielded by research among the private papers of bo
60. ingle layer of stone, some four metres thick, has
    yielded fourteen different species of dinosaur
61. rol talks between the Americans and the Russians
    yielded no results. He felt that his credibility

62. o rotten, and now so tinder-dry that whole limbs
    yielded passionately to the yellow flames that pou
63. more difficult to proceed; for the cattle droves
    yielded place then to mere foot-tracks from weir
64. or Germans-detente was not a useless exercise. It
    yielded positive results, defusing the troubling
65. g for its young. The more complex animals, having
    yielded rigid instinctual behaviour for learning
66. t Roman Catholics lived in Rome, but Barber never
    yielded the point. He was particularly touchy
67. e. I should have guessed that any Russian who had
    yielded to such a capitalist diversionary activi
68. ot only had the wild impulse to go to the Met but
    yielded to it. Not, however, in New York. The
69. r's prospects in Britain. First, the Chancellor
    yielded to his critics and halved the March Budg
70. to him; half-believing the fancy herself, as she
    yielded to his pathetic and inexperienced advances
71. man, any more?' and so life went on. Gemeinschaft
    yielded to Gesellschaft; community was replaced
72. self with outstretched arms as the flesh and bone
    yielded under his weight. Oh god, there was a
73. te redevelopment. Elsewhere Convent Garden has now
    yielded up the market, and argument rages about
74. ours, because although the South African flagpole
    yielded up the ghost easily enough he found when
75. r. She had captured Jocasta now. The intimacy had
    yielded up her own secret. 'No, it's not ugly.
76. d. It had been cultivated the year before but had
    yielded very little. Moumoni said he didn't

yielding
77. men who in 1958 had called him back to Power, by
    yielding Algeria to the Algerian nationalists.
78. f the direct stress (1) now cr. Criteria of
    yielding based on the maximum value of the dri
79. etween the er stresses on the body t: Criteria of
    yielding in that he's asking under the action of
80. wards the main thoroughfare. The crowd was not as
    yielding. The groups of young men called out in
81. ery small ((couple)) here (4) and you will get
    yielding then when the yield stress the average

82. the ((Tresco)) and von ((Meses)) er criteria of
    yielding (3) what are they? (8) Well come on

83. o keep them secret. Pain, terror disorientation,
    yielding absolute loyalty and devotion. The simil

84. as once the masculine province of the area but is
    yielding and its glamour has been somewhat diminis

85. profits back into further investment, thus <p 53>
    yielding further technological advances and further

86. It 'felt' harder because the exhausted soil was
    yielding less, so there was less plant cover for

87. e. Feathers are heavier and cheaper. Foam is less
    yielding, more springy, doesn't last as long as do

88. inevitable. In the meantime, dolphin research is
    yielding new data on the ways in which man's senso

89. t rewriting of his tax program, Mr. Reagan is not
    yielding on his demands for 25 percent cut in pers

90. y is to drive through a car cleaner. The bliss of
    yielding self and car to be soaped, washed and bru

91. 3,200 kilos of wheat per hectare. By 1966, high-
    yielding strain of wheat had been developed that

92. old breeze across the oceanic warmths of the ever
    yielding sub-continent. Even his shabby clothes

93. ishments in St. James's began the slow process of
    yielding to clubs and commerce. I have chosen to

94. qual fervour, Premier Sagasta was progressively
    yielding to American demands and the diplomacy of

95. should at least in part be conceded, or else of
    yielding to extremism what earlier was refused to

96. of this ditch. But all the while, though he kept
    yielding to these invasions of sleep, he could not

yields

97. of new land into cultivation, and an increase in
    yields. But there has been practically no expans

98. an perhaps make this protein in relatively large
    yields. For example, at the moment there are some

99. al more fertilizer than Europe to achieve similar
    yields. In 1975, developed countries used an aver

100. oot zone where they stunt plant growth and reduce
     yields. In the Punjab seepage has raised the wate

101. en, economics supplies only one—whether a thing
     yields a money profit to those who undertake it

102. an activity carried on by a group within society
      yields a profit to society as a whole. Even natio
103. the rents set by a city control board. This board
      yields, about once a year, to the landlords' plea
104. lure to damp down inflationary expectations. Bond
      yields almost everywhere are higher than before
105. oured areas—which were already enjoying higher
      yields and greater wealth than the rest. So the
106. reducing only 80 per cent of the average regional
      yields, and these are low because landlords under
107. ere exported to Turkey, India and Pakistan. Wheat
      yields doubled in India between 1964 and 1972, and
108. ency to permanent cultivation. Where this occurs,
      yields drop to an abysmally low level. As popula-
109. ng to the same patch of ground too frequently, so
      yields fall and the soil is exhausted, sometimes
110. is the spur: poverty may be shared, but when food
      yields fall too low, some of the people on the
111. paddy has gone on producing the same or increased
      yields for centuries, even mill
112. 87 in the cropped area over the last decade, and
      yields have risen by 5 per cent while populat
113. of the soil quickly falls off after clearance—
      yields in the third year may be down to only one
114. ine and more hospitable to cultivated plants. The
      yields in the first year of shifting cultivation
115. wall, a group of Barrier Canyon paintings, still
      yields intriguing detail. A visitor points to
116. of Brompton Road and Thurloe Place Knightsbridge
      yields insensibly to South Kensington.The pave
117. lation grows, or at best a permanent decline in
      yields, irrigated paddy has gone on producing
118. ed acute proportions. At Bangladesh's low average
      yields of half a ton of rice per acre, a man
119. adolescents. Free acting out and talking through
      yields satisfaction. At the same time it
120. tion of components and vastly increased explosive
      yields (such as from fuel air weapons—the
121. hey are allowed to charge. The rent control board
      yields them an extra seven and a half per cent
122. lable means to prevent it. Ovid recommends: 'Love
      yields to business, be employed, you're safe'

123. of nature at the first touch of spirit, before it
     yields to spirit's cosmic venture that we call
124. come self-sufficient by 1956. In 1970 her average
     yields were four times the 1940 levels, reaching
125. ins are late, the growing season is cut short and
     yields will be slashed. Famine and disease follow

Bibliography

Aarts, J. and Meijs, W. (eds.) 1984. *Corpus Linguistics*. Amsterdam: Rodopi.

Austin, J. L. 1962. *How to do things with Words*. London: Oxford University Press.

Benson, J. D., Brainerd, B., and Greaves, W. S. 1986. 'A Quantificational Approach to Field of Discourse', in Brunet, E. and Juillard M. (eds.).

Benson, J. D., Cummings, M. J., and Greaves, W. W. 1988. *Linguistics in a Systemic Perspective*. Toronto: Glendon College, York University.

Biber, D. 1988. *Variation across Speech and Writing*. Cambridge: Cambridge University Press.

Bolivar, A. 1986. *Interaction through written text: a discourse analysis of newspaper editorials*. PhD thesis, University of Birmingham.

Brown, A. F. (ed.) 1963. *Normal and Reverse English word list 1–8*. Philadelphia: University of Pennsylvania.

Brunet, E. and Juillard, M. (eds.) 1986. *Actes du Colloque*. ALLC de Nice, Geneva: Slatkine.

Butler, C. S. 1985. *Systemic Linguistics*: Theory and Application, London: Batsford.

Carter, R. A. 1987. *Vocabulary: Applied Linguistic Perspectives*. London: Allen and Unwin.

Carter, R. A. and McCarthy M. J. (eds.) 1988. *Vocabulary and Language Teaching*. London: Longman.

Clear, J. H. 1987. 'Trawling the Language: Monitor Corpora', in Snell-Hornby (ed.).

Firth, J. R. 1957. *Papers in Linguistics*. London: Oxford University Press.

Garside, R., Leech, G., and Sampson, G. (eds.) 1987. *The Computational Analysis of English*. London: Longman.

Halliday, M. A. K. and Hasan, R. 1976. *Cohesion in English*. London: Longman.

Hanks, P. W. *et al.* 1979. *Collins English Dictionary*. London and Glasgow: Collins.

Hanks, P. W. 1987. 'Definitions and Explanations' in Sinclair, J. M. (ed.) 1987.

Hartmann, R. R. K. (ed.) 1984. *LEXeter '83 Proceedings*. (Lexicographica Series Maior). Tübingen: Niemayer.

Hofland, K. and Johansson, S. 1982. *Word Frequencies in British and American English*. Bergen: The Norwegian Computing Centre for the Humanities.

Ilson, R. (ed.) 1985. *Dictionaries, Lexicography and Language Learning*. (ELT Documents 120) Oxford: Pergamon Press.

Jespersen, O. 1909; 1949. *A Modern English Grammar*. London: Allen and Unwin.

Johansson, S. 1982. *Computer Corpora in English Language Research*. Bergen: Norwegian Computing Centre for the Humanities.

Johansson, S. 1985. *A survey of computer-based English language research*. ICAME News.

Johns, T. F. 1982. 'Exploratory CAL: an Alternative Use of the Computer in the Teaching of English as a Foreign Language', mimeo.

Jones, S. and Sinclair, J. M. 1974. English Lexical Collocations' in *Cahiers de Lexicologie*. 24/15–61.

Kjellmer, G. 1984. 'Why Great: Greatly but not Big: Bigly?', Studia Linguistica 38/ 1–19.

Kjellmer, G. 1984. 'Some thoughts on collocational distinctiveness' in Aarts, J. and Meijs W. (eds.).

Bibliography

Kučera, H. and Francis, W. 1967. *Computational Analysis of Present-Day American English*. Providence, Rhode Island: Brown University Press.

Leech, G. N. and Candlin, C. (eds.) 1986. *Computers in English Language Teaching and Research*. London: Longman.

Leitner, G. (ed.) 1986. *The English Reference Grammar*. Tübingen: Niemayer.

McCarthy, M. J. 1988. 'Some vocabulary patterns in conversation', in Carter, R. A. and McCarthy, M. J. (eds.).

McCarthy, M. J. (ed.) 1988. *Naturalness in Language*. English Language Research Journal Vol. 2. University of Birmingham.

Mindt, D. 1986. 'Corpus, Grammar and Teaching English as a foreign language', in Leitner G. (ed.).

Mindt, D. (ed.) 1988. *Schule und Forschung*. Frankfurt: Diesterweg.

Murray, A. H. *et al.* 1933. *Oxford English Dictionary*. Oxford: Clarendon Press.

Phillips, M. 1983. *Lexical Macrostructure in Science Text*. PhD thesis, University of Birmingham.

Phillips, M. 1985. *Aspects of text structure*. Amsterdam: Elsevier/North-Holland.

Phillips, M. 1989. *Lexical structure of text*. (Discourse Analysis Monographs, 12: English Language Research). University of Birmingham.

Quirk, R., Greenbaum, S., Leech, G. N., Svartvik, J. 1985. *A Comprehensive Grammar of the English Language*. London: Longman.

Reed, A. 1977. 'CLOC: A Collocation Package'. ALLC Bulletin 5.

Renouf, A. 1984. 'Corpus development at Birmingham University', in Aarts, J. and Meijs, W. (eds.).

Renouf, A. 1987. 'Corpus Development', in Sinclair, J. M. (ed.) 1987.

Roe, P. 1977. *The Notion of Difficulty in Scientific Text*. PhD thesis, University of Birmingham.

Sinclair, J. M. 1984. 'Naturalness in Language', in Aarts, J. and Meijs, W. (eds.).

Sinclair, J. M. 1984. 'Lexicography as an Academic Subject', in Hartmann, R. R. K. (ed.).

Sinclair, J. M. 1985. 'Lexicographic Evidence', in R. Ilson (ed.).

Sinclair, J. M., Jones, S., and Daley, R. 1970. *English Lexical Studies*. OSTI Report.

Sinclair, J. M. *et al.* 1987. *Collins COBUILD English Language Dictionary*. London: Collins.

Sinclair, J. M. (ed.) 1987. *Looking Up*. London: Collins.

Sinclair, J. M., Fox, G. *et al.* 1988. *Collins COBUILD Essential English Dictionary*. London: Collins.

Sinclair, J. M., Moon, R. *et al.* 1989. *Collins COBUILD Dictionary of Phrasal Verbs*. London: Collins.

Sinclair, J. M., Moon, R. *et al.* 1990. *Collins COBUILD Student's Dictionary*. London: Collins.

Sinclair, J. M., Fox, G. *et al.* 1990. *Collins COBUILD English Grammar*. London: Collins.

Sinclair, J. M. *et al.* (forthcoming). *English Words in Use*. London: Collins.

Snell-Hornby, M. (ed.) 1987. *ZuriLEX Proceedings*. Tübingen: Francke.

Stock, P. F. 1984. 'Polysemy', in Hartmann, R.R.K. (ed.).

Svartvik, J. (ed.) 1990. *The London–Lund Corpus of Spoken English*. Lund: Lund University Press.

Svartvik, J. and Quirk, R. (eds.) 1980. *A Corpus of English Conversation*. Lund Studies in English 63.

Thomson, A. J. and Martinet, A. V. 1986. *A Practical English Grammar*. Oxford: Oxford University Press.

Willis, J. D. 1990. *The Lexical Syllabus*. London: Collins.

Yang, H. Z. 1986. *A new technique for identifying scientific/technical terms and describing science texts*. Literary and Linguistic Computing 1, no 2: 93–103.

Zipf, G. K. 1935. *The Psychobiology of Language*. Boston: Houghton Mifflin.

Glossary

character
This is a term used in computing to mean roughly a letter of an alphabet; but a set of characters includes punctuation marks and on computer keyboards some shapes that are not found in ordinary typing or printing.

citation
A citation is a selected example of a word or phrase in use. The term comes from lexicography, and citations form the basic evidence for most major dictionaries. A citation can be drawn from the spoken or the written language, and it consists of a word or phrase in a sufficient textual environment to show some feature of its meaning or use.

A set of citations of one particular word or phrase is similar to a concordance (q.v.). However, citations are usually selected by people because of an interesting feature of the occurrence, and so they lack the objectivity of a concordance. From now on, it is likely that new dictionaries will be based on concordances.

Older original dictionaries are based on collections of citations, and the collections can become very large over the years. A collection of citations gives important evidence about a language but should not be confused with a corpus (q.v.), which is a set of representative texts.

Cobuild
Cobuild is an acronym for COllins Birmingham University International Language Database. This is a joint project between industry (Collins Publishers) and the University of Birmingham, which began in 1980. A large corpus of contemporary English was gathered from spoken and written sources, and each word in turn was studied for its lexical, grammatical, semantic, stylistic, and pragmatic features. The information was entered into a database from which were edited the Cobuild dictionaries and other publications. For further information on Cobuild see *Looking Up* (Sinclair (ed.) 1988).

collocate

A word which occurs in close proximity to a word under investigation is called a collocate of it.

collocation

Collocation is the occurrence of two or more words within a short space of each other in a text. The usual measure of proximity is a maximum of four words intervening. Collocations can be dramatic and interesting because unexpected, or they can be important in the lexical structure of the language because of being frequently repeated.

This second kind of collocation, often related to measures of statistical significance, is the one that is usually meant in linguistic discussions. There are three useful technical terms in the description of a collocation. Each citation (q.v.) or concordance (q.v.) line exemplifies a particular word or phrase. This word or phrase is called the node (q.v.). It is normally presented with other words to the left and right and these are called collocates (q.v.). The collocates can be counted and this measurement is called the span (q.v.).

Collocation in its purest sense, as used in this book, recognizes only the lexical co-occurrence of words. This kind of patterning is often associated with grammatical choices as well, leading to the wealth of idioms and fixed phrases that are found in everyday English. Some writers on collocation (e.g. Kjellmer 1982) include matters of grammatical relations in their specification of collocation.

In this book, the attention is concentrated on lexical co-occurrence, more or less independently of grammatical pattern or positional relationship. In most of the examples, collocation patterns are restricted to pairs of words, but there is no theoretical restriction to the number of words involved. Collocation is a contributing factor to idiom (q.v.).

concordance

A concordance is an index to the words in a text. The concordance is at the centre of corpus linguistics, because it gives access to many important language patterns in texts. Concordances to major works such as the Bible and Shakespeare have been available for many years; an example of a concordance is given in Appendix II.

The computer has made concordances easy to compile, and for some thirty years a simple and effective convention called KWIC (Key Word In Context) (q.v.) has been widely used.

The computer-generated concordance can be very flexible; the context of a word can be selected on various criteria (for example counting the words on either side, or finding the sentence boundaries).

Also, sets of examples can be ordered in various ways, see Appendix I, Figures 8, 9, 10, and 11.

context

This key term in modern linguistics has two related meanings:

a. In any continuous text, the words that come on either side of a word or phrase selected for study constitute the context of that word or phrase. In this sense, the context means the linguistic environment of any expression under scrutiny.

Sometimes, to distinguish this meaning from the other, the term co-text (q.v.) is used. In lexical studies, a measured piece of verbal context is called a span (q.v.).

b. The general, non-linguistic environment of any language activity can also be called its context. Here, it means the sociocultural background. Some theories of language, notably Firth (1987), use context or 'context of situation', to mean a level of language description where the limitless complexity of the nonlinguistic environment is organized into linguistically relevant categories.

In many instances of its usage in this book, the above distinction is not very important, and context can be assumed to mean normally the surrounding language, but not necessarily excluding the nonlinguistic environment.

corpus

A corpus is a collection of naturally-occurring language text, chosen to characterize a state or variety of a language. In modern computational linguistics, a corpus typically contains many millions of words: this is because it is recognized that the creativity of natural language leads to such immense variety of expression that it is difficult to isolate the recurrent patterns that are the clues to the lexical structure of the language.

There are two kinds of corpora described in this book. The first is the 'sample corpus', which is a finite collection of texts, often chosen with great care and studied in detail. Once a sample corpus is established, it is not added to or changed in any way.

The other kind of corpus is just beginning to take shape: this is the 'monitor corpus', which re-uses language text that has been prepared in machine-readable form for other purposes—for typesetters of newspapers, magazines, books, and, increasingly, word-processors; and the spoken language mainly for legal or bureaucratic reasons. Chapter 1 gives an account of different corpora.

co-text
The co-text of a selected word or phrase consists of the other words on either side of it. This is a more precise term than context (q.v.) or verbal context, but it is not much used. In Chapter 9, it is developed into a technical term.

discourse
Discourse means language in use—naturally-occurring spoken or written language. In this book it means much the same as text (q.v.); but it is not usually found as a countable noun. It is sometimes used as a very general form for language patterns above the sentence. To some people, discourse suggests the spoken form of the language, and text the written form; in this book, no such distinction is made.

idiom
An idiom is a group of two or more words which are chosen together in order to produce a specific meaning or effect in speech or writing. The word is used in various other ways, but in this book the meaning is restricted to the above.

The individual words which constitute idioms are not reliably meaningful in themselves, because the whole idiom is required to produce the meaning. Idioms overlap with collocations, because they both involve the selection of two or more words. At present, the line between them is not clear. In principle, we call co-occurrences idioms if we interpret the co-occurrence as giving a single unit of meaning. If we interpret the occurrence as the selection of two related words, each of which keeps some meaning of its own, we call it a collocation.

Hence, *hold talks, hold a meeting, hold an enquiry* are collocations; whereas *hold sway, hold the whip hand* are idioms. If either *hold* or *sway* are removed, the special meaning disappears. Most current uses of *sway* as a noun are with *hold*, and the two words must be taken together. Similarly, in *hold the whip hand* nothing can be changed except the inflection of the verb. Other idioms, like *hold ... to ransom*, can be discontinuous.

idiom principle
One of the main principles of the organization of language is that the choice of one word affects the choice of others in its vicinity. Collocation (q.v.) is one of the patterns of mutual choice, and idiom (q.v.) is another. The name given to this principle of organization is the idiom principle.

The other main principle of organization which contrasts with the idiom principle is the open-choice principle (q.v.). The full discussion can be found in Chapter 8.

KWIC
This acronym stands for **Key Word In Context**. It is a popular type of computer-generated concordance, which is easy for a researcher to scan quickly.

Each line of concordance contains an instance of a selected word, and the page is aligned centrally around this word. The text before and after the selected word is printed, then an additional space, the word in question, and more text, until the end of the line is reached. Simple versions of this layout start and stop at the line ends, in the middle of words where necessary. There are several examples of KWIC concordances in the Appendices, notably Appendix II.

lemma
A lemma is what we normally mean by a 'word'. Many words in English have several actual word-forms (q.v.)—so that, for example, the verb *to give* has the forms *give, gives, given, gave, giving,* and *to give.* In other languages, the range of forms can be ten or more, and even hundreds. So 'the word *give*' can mean either (i) the four letters **g, i, v, e,** or (ii) the six forms listed above.

In linguistics and lexicography we have to keep these meanings separate; otherwise it would not be possible to understand a sentence like '*Give* occurs 50 times in this text'. For this reason, the composite set of word-forms is called the lemma.

lemmatization
(See *lemma* and *word-form*.) Lemmatization is the process of gathering word-forms and arranging them into lemmas or lemmata. So the

word-forms *give, gives, gave, given, giving*, and probably *to give*, will conventionally be lemmatized into the lemma *give*. Any occurrence of any of the six forms will be regarded as an occurrence of the lemma. There are a number of problems about lemmatization, because there are so many possible ways of grouping word-forms. Most books about linguistics assume that lemmatization is a simple and obvious process, especially in a language such as English. However, a lot of research is still needed to justify lemmatization on scientific grounds.

lexis, lexical

The lexis of a language is the set of all its word-forms (q.v.). Lexical structure is the organization of these word-forms into units such as collocations (q.v.) and idioms (q.v.).

The origins of lexical evidence are the word-patterns in texts. Position and frequency of occurrence are important criteria, and in the first instance priority is given to the formal arrangements of word-forms, rather than to intuitive conclusions about meaning.

This distinguishes lexis from semantics, which is centrally concerned with the organization of meaning. However, lexical study aims to associate the formal patterns with distinctions in meaning, and so lexis and semantics overlap.

Sometimes lexis is contrasted with grammar, and in this kind of usage it emphasizes the individual patterns of words as against the generalizations of grammatical rules.

naturalness

Competent users of a language acquire acute sensitivity to naturally-occurring language, and are quite good at spotting contrived and artificial constructions. At present, it is beyond the competence of linguistic research to describe this facility, and we must conclude that the phraseology of language in text is more subtly organized than we can express or explain.

There is an edition of the English Language Research Journal (McCarthy, (ed.) 1988, vol. 2) which puts the case very clearly and explores some of the consequences of this observation. In relation to the concerns of this book, naturalness reinforces the insistence on working only from attested examples of language. Many writers and teachers have found it convenient to argue from pieces of invented or adapted language; increasingly this is becoming a hazardous occupation and before long it will be abandoned altogether.

Naturalness is to text what grammatical correctness is to sentences. The two principles come close together and indeed overlap; but whereas most educated people have been taught the conventions of grammatical correctness, they have not approached text with the same rigour. They do not have a ready vocabulary for talking about textual well-formedness, but they are aware of its influence on the success of both spoken and written language in practice.

node
The node word in a collocation (q.v.) is the one whose lexical behaviour is under examination.

open-choice principle
In many descriptions of language—grammars and dictionaries especially—words are treated as independent items of meaning. Each of them represents a separate choice. Collocations (q.v.), idioms (q.v.), and other exceptions to this principle are given lower status in the descriptions.

This is the open-choice principle, which contrasts with the idiom principle (q.v.). A full discussion can be found in Chapter 8.

running words
This term is used in measuring the length of a text. Each successive word-form (q.v.) is counted once, whether or not that particular form has occurred before. For example, the phrase 'The wind in the willows' contains 5 running words. Contrast this with vocabulary (q.v.).

span
This is the measurement, in words, of the co-text (q.v.) of a word selected for study. A span of −4, +4 means that four words on either side of the node (q.v.) word will be taken to be its relevant verbal environment. (See *collocation*).

text
This word can be used as a countable noun or uncountable noun.

a. A text is a complete and continuous piece of spoken or written language. Note that spoken text is included.
b. Text is continuous spoken or written language. In this book, it usually refers to such language in machine-readable form.

Note that there is little if any difference in meaning between text and discourse (q.v.).

vocabulary
The vocabulary of a text is the set of all the different words used in the text. Vocabulary is usually counted in lemmas (q.v.) and contrasted with the count of running words (q.v.).

For example the phrase 'The wind in the willows' contains 5 running words, but its vocabulary has only 4 items since *the* occurs twice.

All the words of a text are part of its vocabulary—even the very common words such as *the, of, and*, which are sometimes said to be restricted to the grammar.

word
It is best to use the word *word* informally to mean what it normally means. Roughly speaking a word in the Roman alphabet is based on a string of letters including hyphen and sometimes apostrophe—bounded on each side by a word space or another punctuation mark. It can thus signify anything from a word-form (q.v.) to a lemma (q.v.), from a running word (q.v.) to a vocabulary (q.v.) word. This is a large range of variation, and the use of the term is not very precise. However 'word' is used for one of the basic concepts of language. The concept is sometimes expressed as 'minimum free form'; simultaneously the unit of vocabulary and the smallest unit of syntax.

word-form
This term is used for any unique string of characters, bounded by spaces. Hence *give, giving, gave, given* are all separate word-forms. (See *lemma*).

Index

Entries relate to the Introduction, Chapters 1 to 9, and the glossary. References to the glossary are indicated by 'g' after the page number.